Rhythm Guitar
The Complete Guide

by Bruce Buckingham
& Eric Pascal

ISBN 0-7935-8184-2

7777 W. BLUEMOUND RD. P.O. BOX 13819 MILWAUKEE, WI 53213

Visit Hal Leonard Online at
www.halleonard.com

Table of Contents

Introduction

The art and craft of good rhythm guitar playing is not always taught or practiced correctly by all guitarists. It is the aim of this Rhythm Guitar curriculum to give you the tools and inspiration to study and play "rhythm" with knowledge and conviction.

Fundamentals are always important to technique and the reviewing of material is mandatory. This curriculum starts simply and progresses to advanced topics, but it must be stressed that the learning of the material has to go hand in hand with the "playing" of the material. This is achieved through disciplined practice and creative application in performance.

You need to practice the material well enough so you can perform all examples and playing techniques. Repetition in practice and performance makes solid rhythm guitar. Regardless of your level of chord knowledge or experience in playing rhythm guitar, this book will serve as an "idea source" from which you can invent your own sounds. Remember that anything can go anywhere using the right approach and your ears.

We recommend that you also refer to other Musician's Institute books, *Single String Technique* (by Dan Gilbert and Beth Marlis) and *Music Reading for Guitar* (by David Oakes); which put forth and define many of the fingerboard and rhythmic applications used in this book. It is also a good idea to seek the advice of a local teacher that can check your progress and help you over any rough spots.

Finally, a word about *practicing:* Use a metronome and/or drum machine when learning examples and practice all progressions at a variety of tempos. Also, be creative in the use of all your learning tools (Tapes, books, videos, sequencer, CD's). Try and build a repertoire of progressions and songs. Write your own progressions and songs. The more creative you become in your approach to chords, the easier the shapes will become.

Chapter One

1

Objectives

- To understand diagrams used in chord shapes.
- To learn proper fretting hand placement.
- To learn major and minor open position chords for the seven "roots" (A–B–C–D–E–F–G).
- To learn basic strumming technique and rhythmic control exercises.
- To play "basic moves."

The Diagram

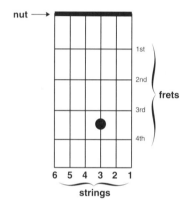

This *vertical diagram* is the most commonly used diagram for guitar. It is used to show the first four or five frets starting at the nut. The frets are actually the metal wires. However, the "fret area" (the space between the nut and fret, or from one fret to the next) is generally referred to as the "fret." Frets are numbered from #1 as the lowest, all the way up the neck to the highest.

Sometimes a numeral will be used at the lowest fret in the diagram to indicate a different starting fret other than the first fret. This way, you can use this diagram to show any four or five consecutive frets on the guitar.

The strings are also numbered. The highest-pitched string is #1 and the lowest-pitched string is #6. The note pictured to the right is the *"third string, fourth fret."* It is important to be able to find any location on the neck described in this manner.

Open Position Major Chords

The first seven chords we will learn are major triads, built from the seven natural notes: A–B–C–D–E–F–G.

These are termed *natural* because they have no sharps (♯) or flats (♭) in combination with the letter name. The letter is also called the *root*. The root gives the chord its name and is also the 1st note in the major scale of the chord.

- Place the fingers of the fretting hand just behind the metal fret wires, so the finger is in the front half of the fret area.
- Use the tops of the fingers (fingertips).
- Place thumb behind neck at the second fret.
- Practice all seven shapes and memorize them.

* ⦿ = Root throughout this entire book.

"Basic Moves"

"Basic moves" are short combinations of chords (two or three) that are typical movements of chord shapes found inside longer chord progressions and songs. These are meant to be practiced on a daily basis in order to make the transition from one chord to another an automatic response. Repetition, patience, and observation of the fretting hand are mandatory to make every move easy.

The repeat sign (:‖) means to repeat the preceding section. Generally, a repeat sign indicates to play that section a total of *two times.* However, a direction such as "play 4 times" can alter the number of repeats to be played. For these exercises, play 4 times as a minimum, and eventually work up your endurance to 8 times on each.

- Practice these progressions slowly and cleanly before speeding up.
- Play with downstrokes of the pick on each beat, counting out loud, "one…two…three…four."
- Each "hash mark" represents one beat.

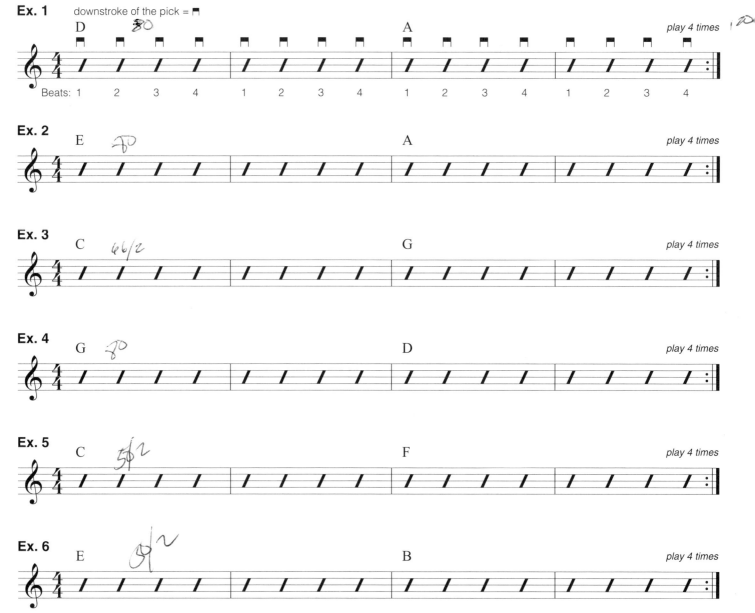

Also practice these "basic moves" with only four beats per chord (1 bar). Then, try two beats per chord. Listen to the chords closely to obtain a clear tone.

Open Position Minor Chords

Here are the seven "natural-note" minor triads:

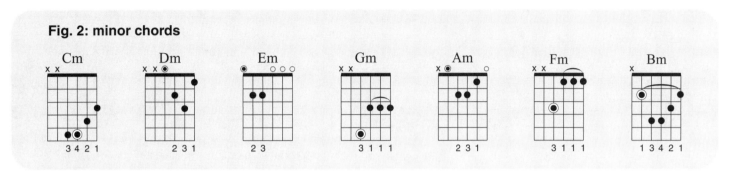

Fig. 2: minor chords

Cm Dm Em Gm Am Fm Bm

More "Basic Moves"

Play the following "basic moves" for minor triads:

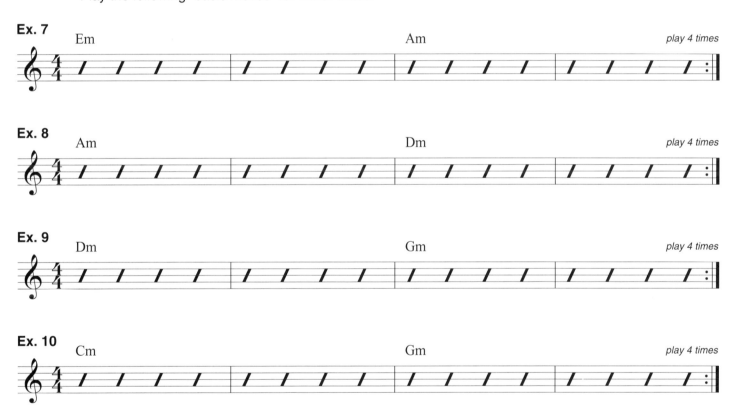

Ex. 7 Em Am *play 4 times*

Ex. 8 Am Dm *play 4 times*

Ex. 9 Dm Gm *play 4 times*

Ex. 10 Cm Gm *play 4 times*

Now let's combine both major and minor chords.

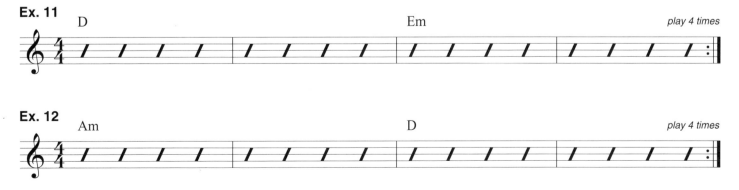

Ex. 11 D Em *play 4 times*

Ex. 12 Am D *play 4 times*

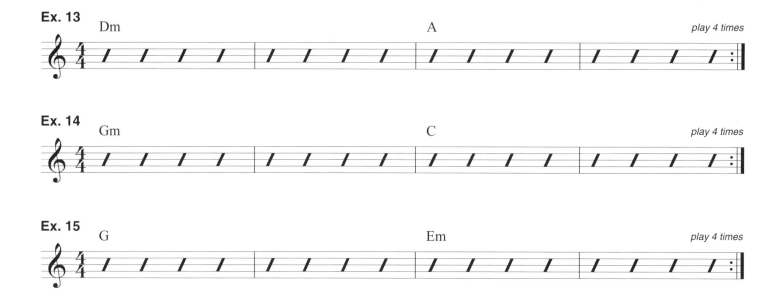

Ex. 13 Dm   A   *play 4 times*

Ex. 14 Gm   C   *play 4 times*

Ex. 15 G   Em   *play 4 times*

Remember:

- Repetition and relaxation.
- Eventually, play eight times through each set of chords.

Strumming and Rhythmic Control

Learning to strum relaxed and steady with the beat is your connection with the rhythm of a piece of music. If you feel the least bit awkward in either hand (but especially the strumming hand), the music won't groove. Always strive to keep your foot tapping and your strumming hand relaxed. *Hear the time! Use a metronome!*

We will concentrate on playing quarter note and eighth note rhythm patterns as shown in examples 16-20 below. Strum muted strings to start.

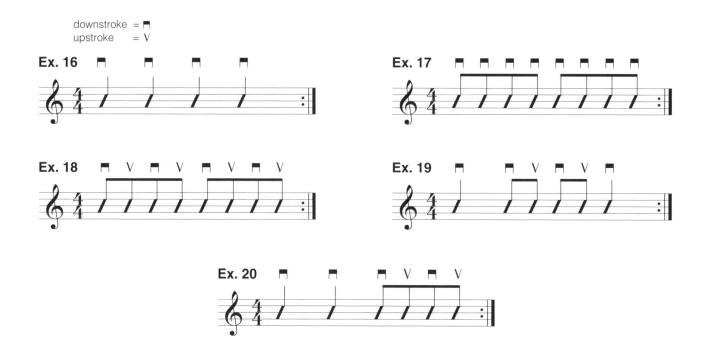

Now, try applying these rhythms to chords. Hear the quarter note pulse and the eighth note subdivision of the beat.

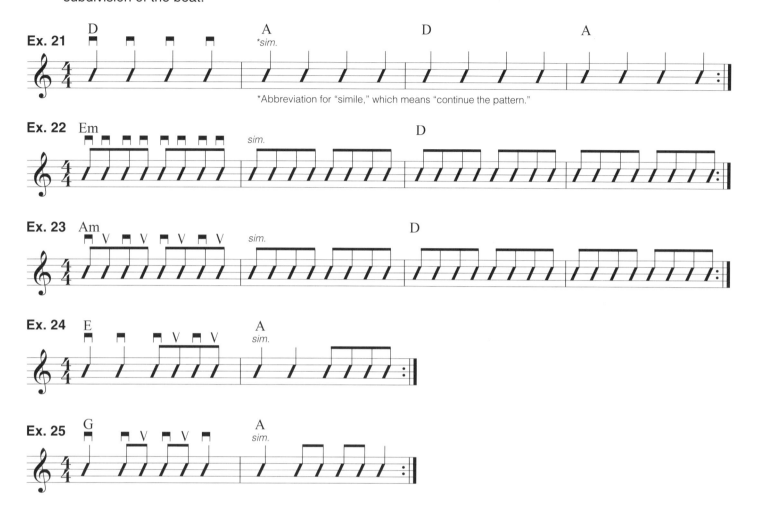

*Abbreviation for "simile," which means "continue the pattern."

Progressions

Progressions are combinations of chords repeated in a pattern. They usually contain a key *center* that defines their sound. It is invaluable to be able to play common progressions and recognize their "key centers" by ear while playing.

The following progressions each have a certain key center. Can you name the I chord? (Answers given on page 10.)

- Practice until the chords flow and the rhythm is flawless.
- Strum all combinations of strums mentioned so far with each progression.
- Vary the tempo of each progression (slow-fast).
- Stay on the tips of the fingers in the front half of the fret area.

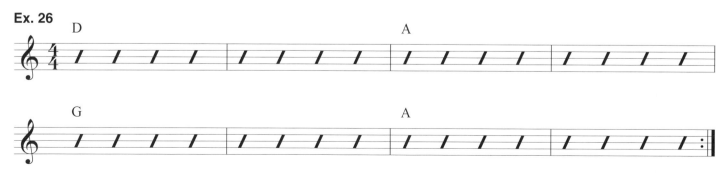

- Regular reveiw is a must.
- Make up your own progressions.

Key centers: Ex. 26, D–Ex. 27, G–Ex. 28, E–Ex. 29, C–Ex. 30, D–Ex. 31, Am.

Chapter Two

2

Objectives

- To learn dominant 7th open position chords for the seven roots (A–B–C–D–E–F–G).
- To be able to play "basic moves."
- To learn bass note with chord strum technique.
- To play rhythmic control exercises at indicated tempos.

Open Position Chords

The next chord type to work with is the *dominant 7th*. These chords are extremely important in defining "key centers" and, along with the major and minor chords you already learned, they make up the twenty-one open chords that are the backbone of guitar. You will see all of these shapes reappearing further up the neck in the higher positions. Therefore, it is best to become very familiar with these twenty-one shapes in open position so you have a solid foundation in the continuing study of the guitar neck and its intricacies.

Dominant 7th chords

- First, study the seven shapes and get a feel for each.
- Then observe the relationship between the major triad and the dominant 7th chord with the same letter name. Only one note is different! Which string is different?
- Dominant 7ths have four notes in them, one more than major and minor triads. See if you can sing (hear) the "extra" note.

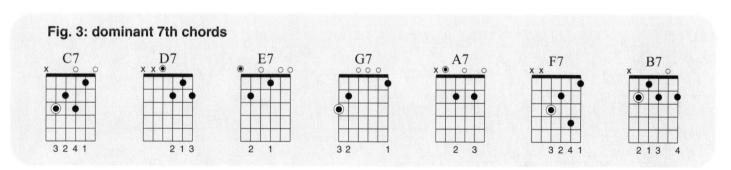

Fig. 3: dominant 7th chords

"Basic moves" with dominant 7th chords only:

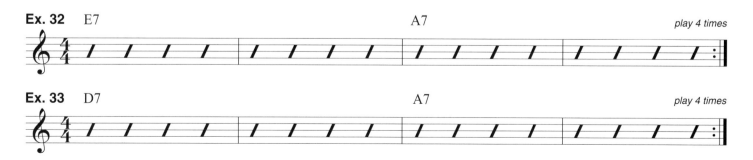

11

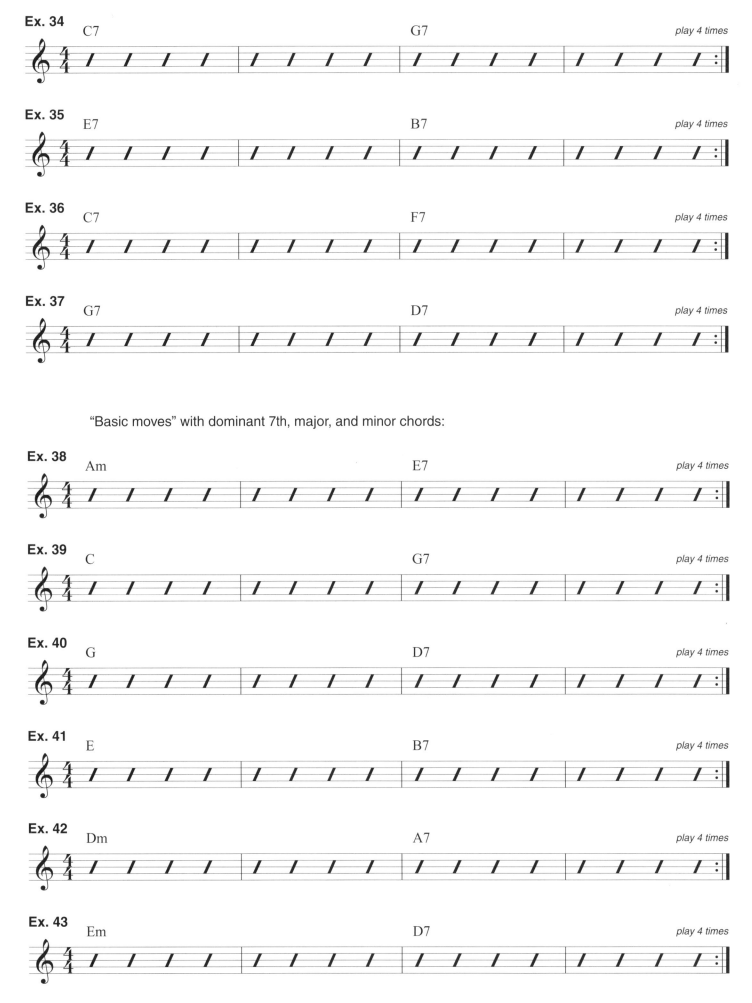

"Basic moves" with dominant 7th, major, and minor chords:

Root/Chord Strumming

The term *root* refers to the note which gives the chord its name. For example, A is the root of A7, and E is the root of Em.

You have learned three types of chords, built on each of the seven roots. That's our twenty-one chords. Learn and memorize where the root is located on each chord shape. Most of the time, the root is the lowest note (also known as the "bass note"). You should be able to clearly pluck the root first, and then follow that with full strumming. The coordination should feel comfortable at many different tempos. Remember to vary your tempos and your strums.

The root/chord type of strum is written like this:

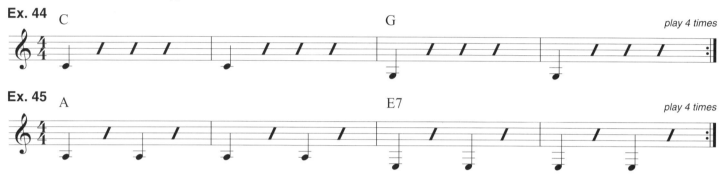

This looks easy, but the ability to execute the bass note cleanly at a variety of tempos and with all chords shapes will only come with repeated practice and a strong emphasis on *time.*

Ex. 46

Add this type of strumming technique to your repertoire and it will improve your overall sense of *time, bass motion,* and *harmony.*

In each of the chords studied so far, the root is the lowest note. Since the location of the root is different for each chord, here's a reference sheet of all the chords studied, with the roots. Study this figure until all chord shapes and root locations are learned. Then write out all the shapes again from memory.

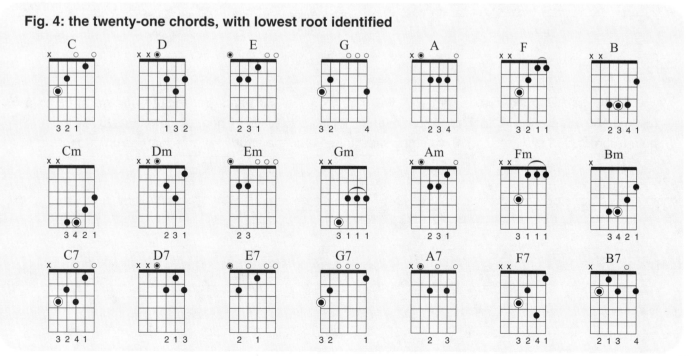

Fig. 4: the twenty-one chords, with lowest root identified

Practice Tips

At this time, the strumming hand (the right hand for most of us) should be discussed. It is very important to work on exercises that develop the dexterity in this hand and promote a strong, confident sense of time. These progressions are meant to be practiced on a daily basis to obtain the desired ability. Here are some things to remember:

- **Dynamics** (loud and soft) should always be a part of your practice.

- **Repetition** is the only way to develop *relaxed* coordination.

- **Tempo** should be varied between progressions from very slow to as fast as possible! Don't stay at the same tempo for the whole practice session!

- **Rhythms** from strumming and fingerpicking can be staccato (short) or legato (long).

Fingerstyle vs. Flatpicking

Some guitarists always use a pick, and some use only their fingers. However, the best approach is to be able to do both. When playing these progressions, try both ways, maybe alternating days in your practice schedule. One day play all progressions with a pick, the next day with your fingers.

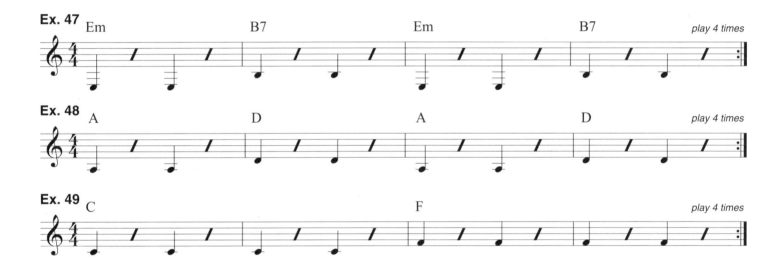

In the following exercises, start with the metronome at 60 beats per minute and get it up to a relaxed 160 beats per minute. First, strum quarter notes as indicated. Then, on beats that follow the root note (represented by *hash* marks), you may substitute one of the strum patterns learned on page 8.

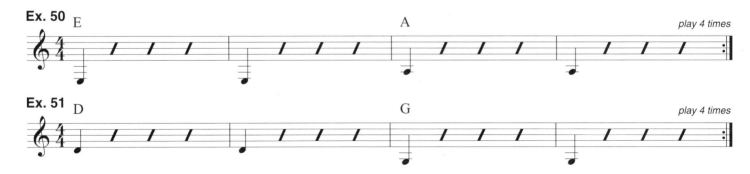

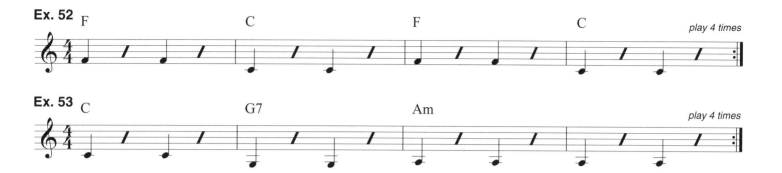

More Strums

Let's look at some strums that have a little *syncopation* within them. For these examples, syncopation refers to the two upbeats in a row. If we tie an upbeat eighth note over to the next eighth note, we will end up with the same upbeat attack played twice in a row. The syncopation occurs on beats 1&2 then on 3&4 then on beats 2&3 in the examples below. It becomes a two-beat rhythm figure that can be played with. The trick is to not let the strumming hand stop going up and down constantly—just *miss* the strings on the downstroke when you want to have two ups in a row. This basic syncopation is found in every style of music and it must feel comfortable at all tempos. The second measure of each example shows the same syncopated rhythm, rewritten with a quarter note to replace the tied eighths (except in example 56, where the syncopation spans the midpoint of the the measure.)

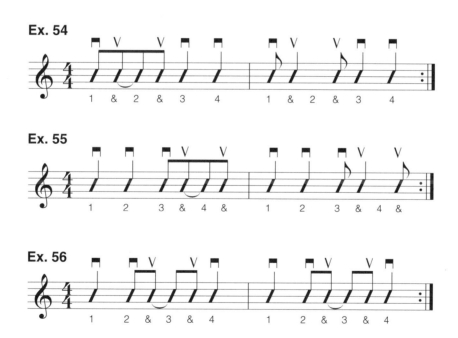

It is important to be able to tap your foot as you play these strums. This basic coordination between the *foot* going down and up, and the *hand* going down and up, is your link to feeling time. First try the new strums with chord pairs (basic moves, page 6) then try the progressions on the next page. Remember to play cleanly in both hands, but don't let the beat slow down, or drag.

Try these progressions at the tempos indicated, and experiment with different strum patterns.

Ex. 57

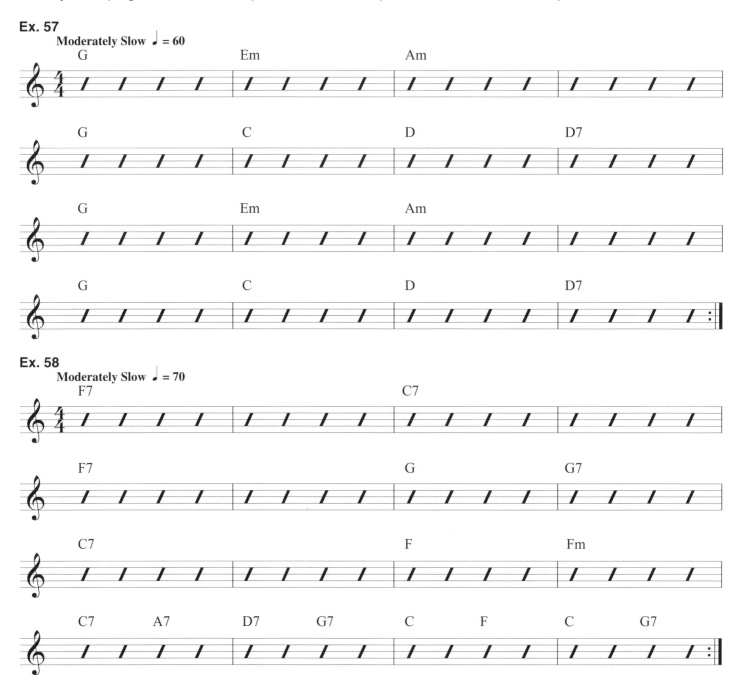

Ex. 58

Notes:

Chapter Three

Objectives

- To learn major and minor barre chord shapes with roots on the sixth and fifth strings.
- To play "basic moves."
- To play progressions using major and minor barre chord shapes.
- To review all rhythm patterns and strums given in chapters one and two.

Barre Chords

Barre chord shapes are movable to any fret on the fingerboard because they contain no open strings. Since we are looking at shapes from sixth and fifth string roots with only major and minor chord types, we need only learn a total of four shapes to play these from any of the twelve roots (A–B–B♭–C–etc.)

In order to get a clean sound from the fretting hand, you should check each string carefully by picking it alone and listening to make sure it is clear and not "buzzing." These shapes might take a while to perfect, but they are the most common chords (after open position) played on the guitar. You must be able to play them with ease and at any tempo. The positioning of the barre finger and the other notes will take some time but you will eventually get the feel of each chord shape. Don't be afraid to "wiggle" your fingers into place to get a good sound. If your fingers aren't placed well on the fingerboard, no amount of pressure will make the chord sound any better.

Barre Chords with Sixth String Roots

Here are the barre chord shapes with a sixth string root. They are built from open-position E major and E minor chord shapes. Notice how these two open position shapes are simply moved up, with the first finger forming the "barre" across the fingerboard.

Fig. 5: major and minor barre chords, with root on the sixth string

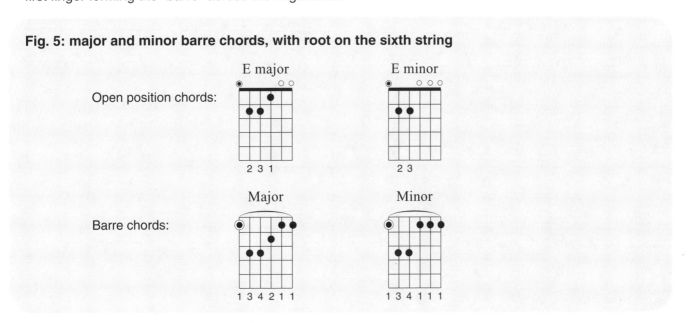

To play specific chords using these barre chord shapes, you'll need to know the names of the notes on the sixth string. (The notes on the first string are exactly the same as on the sixth string.)

Fig 6: notes on the sixth string

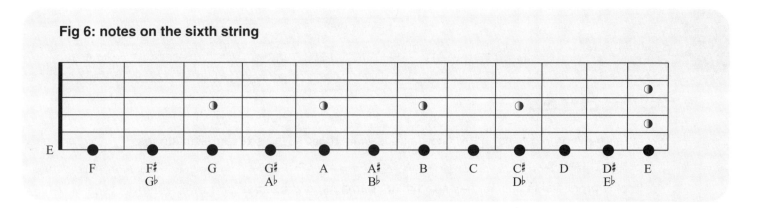

Play these "basic moves" using sixth-string-root barre chords only.

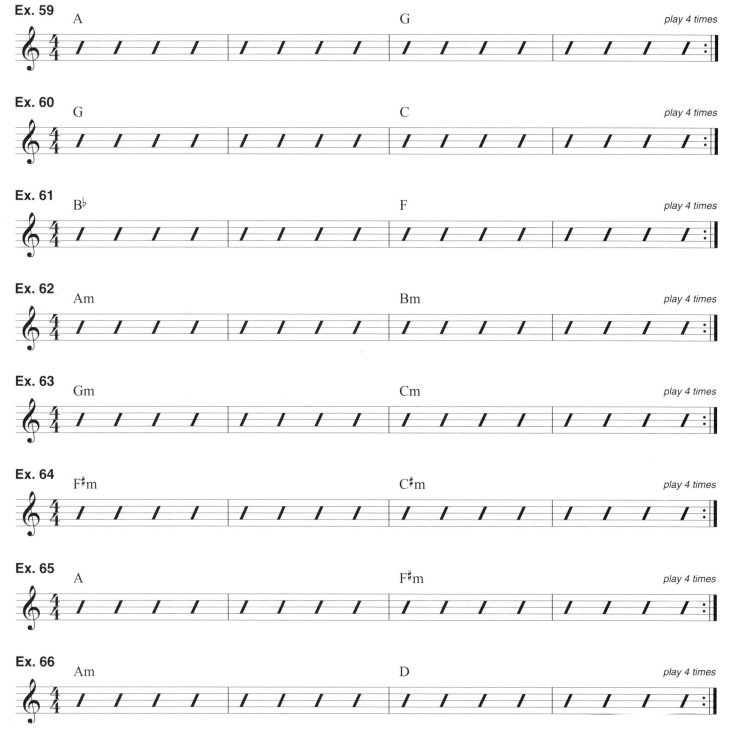

Barre Chords with Fifth String Roots

Here are the barre chord shapes with a fifth string root. They are built from open-position A major and A minor chords. Notice how these two open-position shapes are simply moved up, and the first finger plays the root and the third finger forms the barre on the major shape. An alternate fingering is also shown with the first finger forming the barre and the other notes being played with single fingers. Practice both ways to get the feel of each. The minor shape uses the barre with first finger all the way across the fretboard.

Fig.7: major and minor barre chords, with root on the fifth string

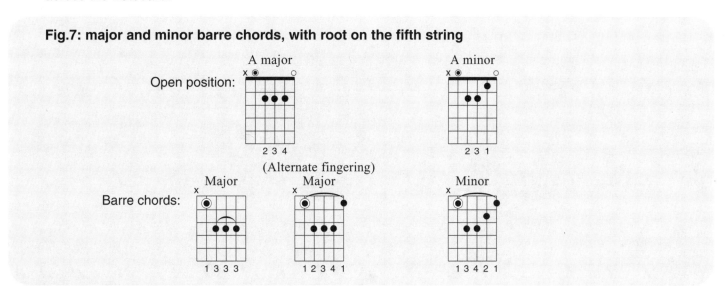

Fig. 8: notes on the fifth string

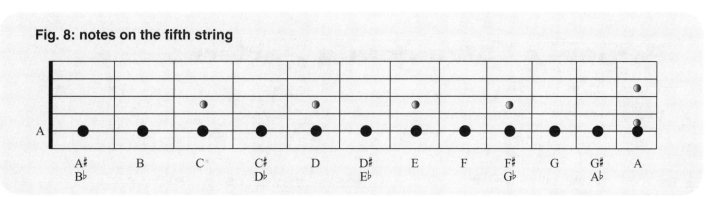

Play these "basic moves" using fifth-string-root barre chords only.

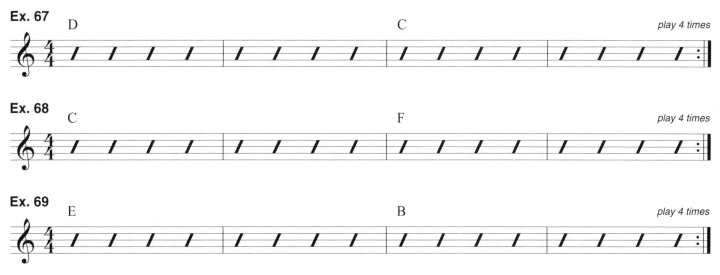

Ex. 67   D   C   *play 4 times*

Ex. 68   C   F   *play 4 times*

Ex. 69   E   B   *play 4 times*

Ex. 70

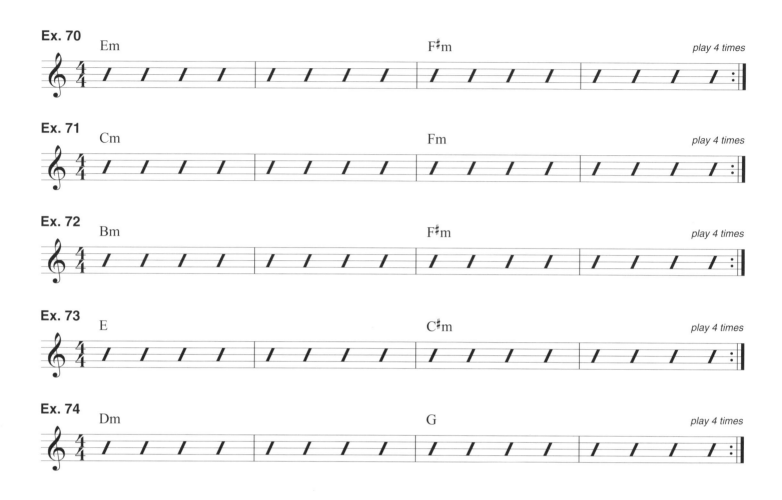

Ex. 71

Ex. 72

Ex. 73

Ex. 74

Review of Strumming Patterns

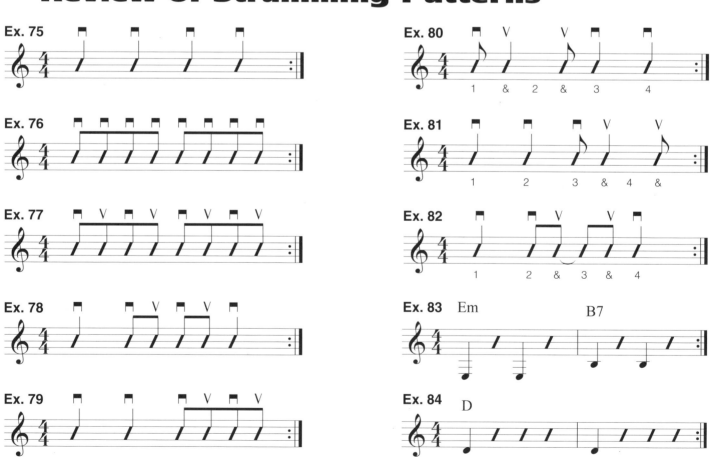

Ex. 75

Ex. 76

Ex. 77

Ex. 78

Ex. 79

Ex. 80

Ex. 81

Ex. 82

Ex. 83

Ex. 84

"Basic Moves"

Next, let's combine fifth- and sixth-string-root barre chords together. The root string (sixth or fifth) is written below each chord symbol, under the staff.

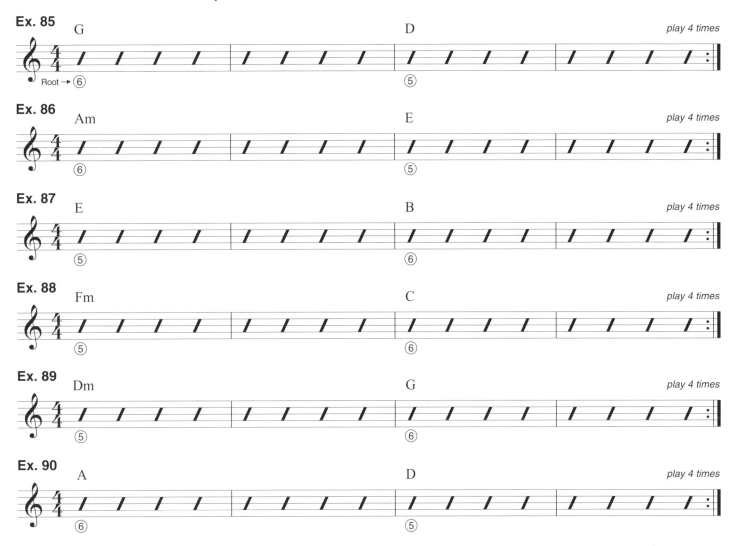

Progressions

Play all chord progressions below and on the next page using only barre chord shapes. The root string (sixth or fifth) is indicated below the staff.

- Practice until the chords flow and the rhythm is flawless.
- Play all strums shown on page 20 with each progression.
- Vary the tempo (slow-fast) of the different progressions.

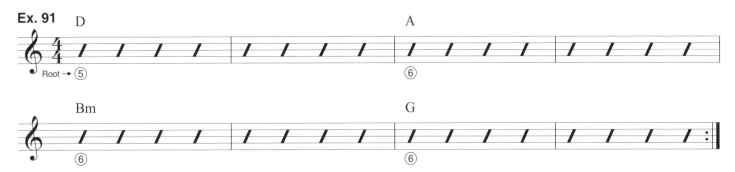

Ex. 92

Ex. 93

Ex. 94

Ex. 95

Notes:

Chapter Four

Objectives

- To learn dominant 7th barre chord shapes with roots on the sixth and fifth strings.
- To play "basic moves."
- To learn and play new rhythm patterns (strums).
- To play progressions using major, minor, and dominant 7th barre chord shapes.

Dominant 7th Barre Chords with Sixth String Roots

In Chapter 3 we learned major and minor shapes for the fifth and sixth strings. Let's continue by adding dominant 7th barre chord shapes with roots on the fifth and sixth strings.

The sixth-string-root dominant 7th barre chord shape is built from the open position E7. Notice how this open position shapes is simply moved up, with the first finger forming the "barre" across the fingerboard.

Fig. 9: dominant 7th shapes, with root on the sixth string

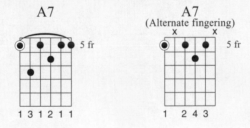

Moveable Shapes

Not all chords that move up and down the neck involve the use of a barre. The alternate A7 shown above is the first one we have learned so far that does not. We will refer to these chords as "moveable chords." You will eventually have many ways to play any chord, and seeing the common tones between different chord shapes that are the same chord is important.

Try to play the following "basic moves" with both of the dominant chord shapes shown above in Figure 9. It may take a while to get them both to sound and feel comfortable, but it is well worth the effort. Use sixth-string-root barre chords only.

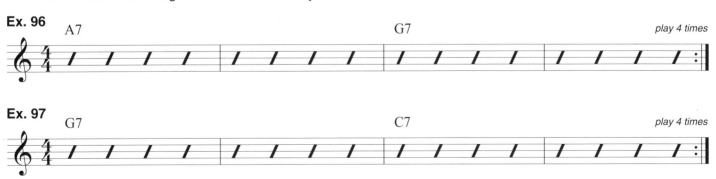

4

Ex. 98

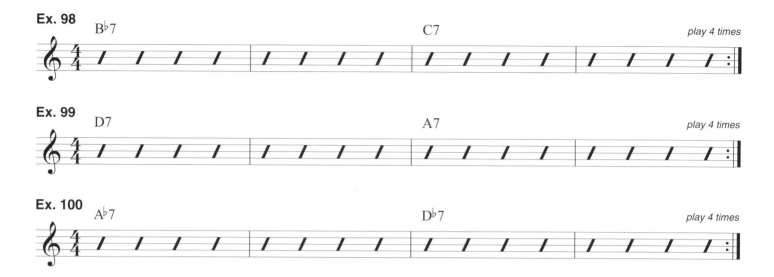

Ex. 99

Ex. 100

Dominant 7th Barre Chords with Fifth String Roots

Here is the fifth string root dominant 7th barre chord shape, which is built from the open position A7. Notice how this open position shape is simply moved up, with the first finger forming the barre from the fifth string across to the first string.

Fig. 10: dominant 7th shapes, with root on the fifth string

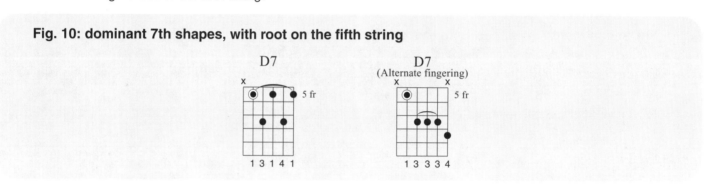

Note: When playing the alternate fingering for the dominant 7th, it is not necessary to barre the first finger; only the third finger should be barred.

Play these "basic moves" using the fifth-string-root barre chords only.

Ex. 101

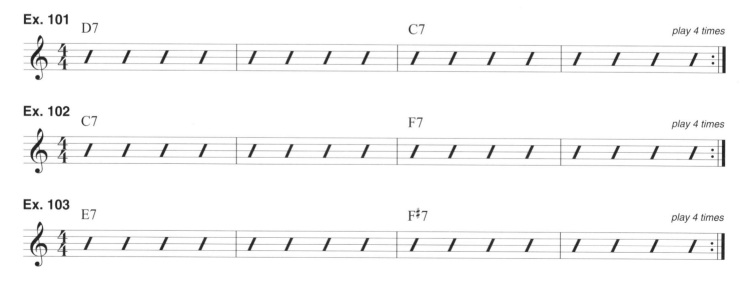

Ex. 102

Ex. 103

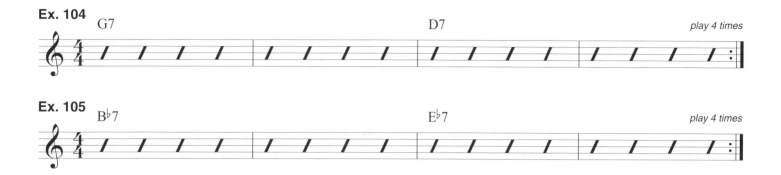

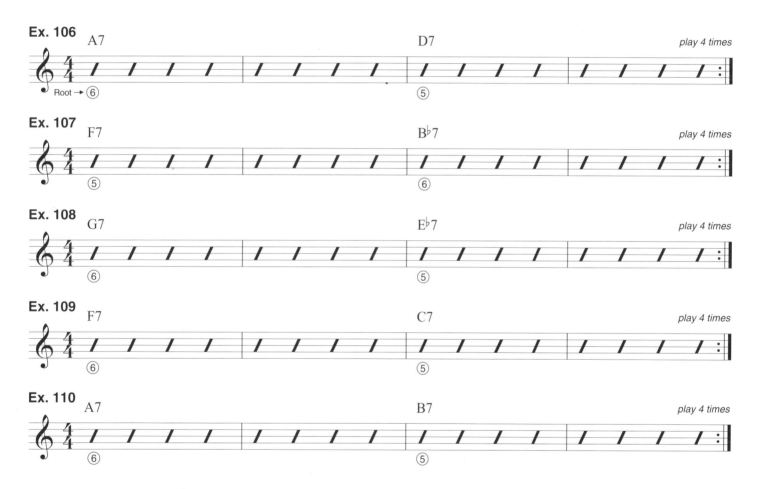

"Basic Moves"

Next, let's combine fifth- and sixth-string dominant 7th barre chords together. The string root is indicated by "6" or "5" below each chord.

Strumming and Rhythmic Control

Let's now add two new rhythm patterns (strums) to the ones you learned in Chapters 1 and 2. Both new rhythm patterns employ a *tie* from the upbeat of "2" to the downbeat of "3". Counting and feeling the eighth notes in these rhythm patterns is essential! Pay close attention to the strumming indications.

Strum muted strings only (no sounding chord) to start.

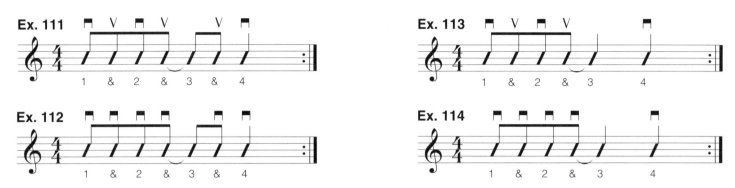

Next let's play these new rhythms with chord changes. Count and feel the eighth notes and pay close attention to down/up pick indications.

This symbol means to repeat the figure in the previous bar.

Progressions

Play the chord progressions on the next page using major, minor, and dominant 7th barre chord shapes only. The string root indications have been left blank except for the starting chord. This time, *you* decide which chord shape is closest to the last one played, and write in the correct string root in each black circle.

- Practice until the chords flow and the rhythm is flawless.

- Play the new rhythm patterns (strums) from page 26 with all progressions.

- Vary the tempo of the progressions (slow to fast).

Chapter Five

5

Objectives

- To learn a variety of arpeggiated rhythm patterns using all the chord shapes learned so far.
- To learn to play "basic moves."
- To learn to play chord progressions using arpeggiated patterns.

Arpeggiated Chords

An *arpeggiated* pattern is one where the notes of a chord are played one at a time, rather than strummed together. There are many different combinations of arpeggiated patterns ranging from simple to complex. Ultimately, you want to be able to improvise an arpeggiated pattern for any given chord progression. Arpeggiated chords can be played fingerstyle, with a flat pick, or with a combination of the two; depending on the pattern and the style being played. Given the situation, you want to become comfortable using any picking method you need. In the following exercises, experiment using fingerstyle, flat pick, and a combination of the two (hybrid picking, with pick and fingers).

Arpeggiated Pattern 1

This pattern involves playing only the *top four strings* of any given chord in ascending direction. The picking order of the strings is 4–3–2–1. When using a flat pick, follow the suggested picking. (NOTE: There are two picking sequences using a flat pick.) Make sure and play all notes legato (let ring).

Fig. 11: arpeggiated pattern 1

Play the following "basic moves," using arpeggiated pattern 1 in eighth notes. The specific chord shapes to use are shown to the right of each example.

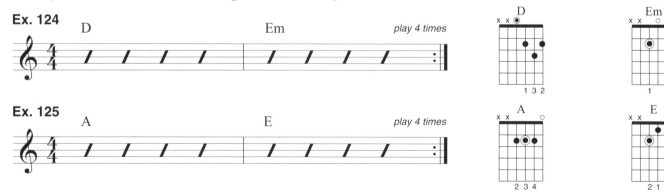

Ex. 126   Dm   A7   *play 4 times*

Arpeggiated Pattern 2

Arpeggiated pattern 2 involves first playing the root note of any given chord (on string 6, 5, or 4) and then playing the top three strings in ascending order. The picking sequence is: Root–string 3–string 2–string 1. When using a flat pick, follow each of the suggested picking directions.

Fig. 12: arpeggiate pattern 2

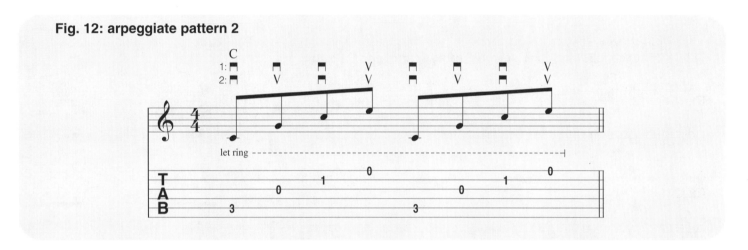

Play the following "basic moves" using arpeggiated Pattern 2.

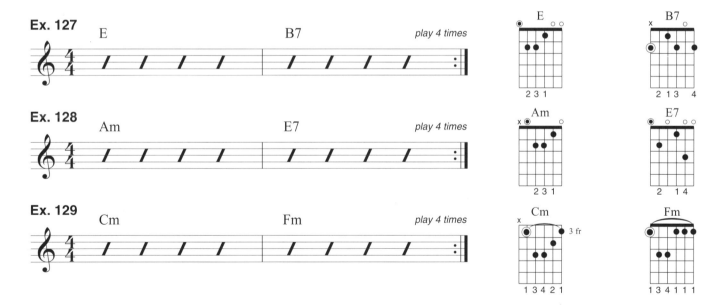

Ex. 127   E   B7   *play 4 times*

Ex. 128   Am   E7   *play 4 times*

Ex. 129   Cm   Fm   *play 4 times*

Arpeggiated Pattern 3

Arpeggiated Pattern 3 involves playing the root of any given chord first (on string 6, 5, or 4), then playing the top three strings in descending order. The picking sequence is: Root–string 1–string 2–string 3. When using flat pick, follow the suggested picking directions.

Fig. 13: arpeggiated pattern 2

Play the following "basic moves" with Arpeggiated Pattern 3.

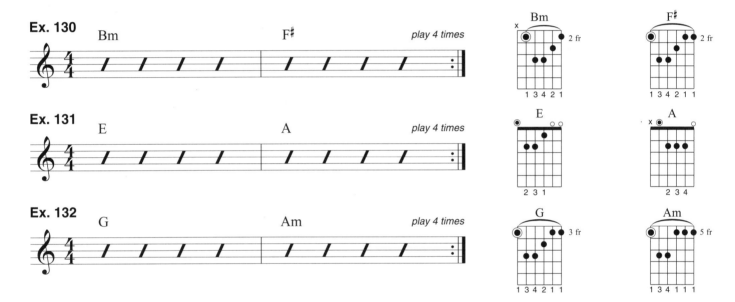

Ex. 130 Bm   F♯   *play 4 times*

Ex. 131 E   A   *play 4 times*

Ex. 132 G   Am   *play 4 times*

Arpeggiated Pattern 4

Arpeggiated Pattern 4 involves playing the root note of any given chord first (on string 6, 5, or 4), and then playing the top three strings in mixed order. The picking sequence is: Root–string 1–string 3–string 2. When using a flat pick, follow the suggested picking direction.

Fig. 14: arpeggiated pattern 4

Play the following "basic moves" with Arpeggiated Pattern 4.

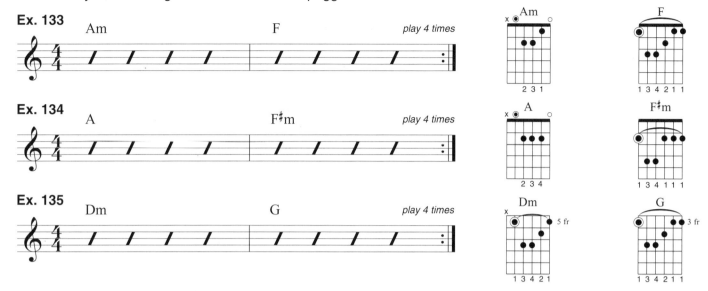

Progressions

Play the following chord progressions using the four arpeggiated patterns learned in this chapter. You choose the exact chord locations.

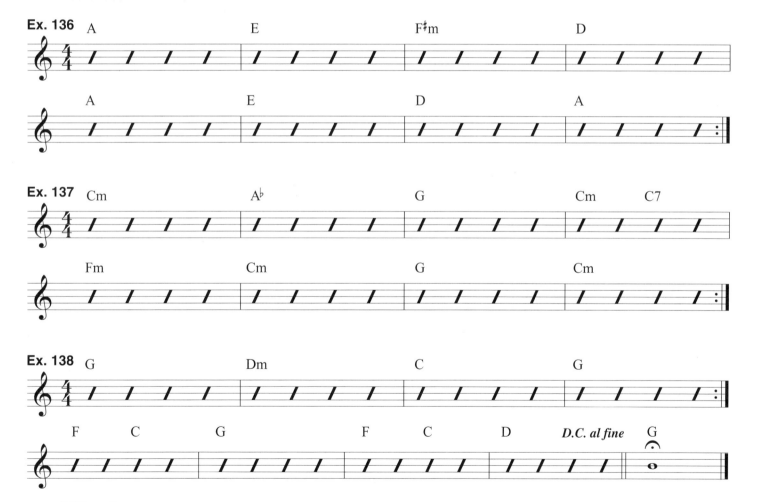

Notes:

Chapter Six

6

Objectives

- To learn "power chord" shapes.
- To play charts containing two rhythm guitar parts.

Although very simple in concept, "power chords" can add depth and interest in many rhythm guitar parts, especially when added to an already existing rhythm guitar part. Power chords offer a way to have two rhythm parts playing, without having the parts get in the way of each other. Since power chords contain only the root and 5th (no 3rd) they can be played over both major and minor chords. In addition, they usually offer a lower timbre than full-voiced chords. Rhythmically, they are generally interpreted differently than full voiced five or six string chords.

Power Chord Shapes

Figure 15 shows power chord shapes with roots on the sixth, fifth and fourth strings.
The written symbol for power chords is A5, E5, C5, etc.

Fig 15: power chord shapes

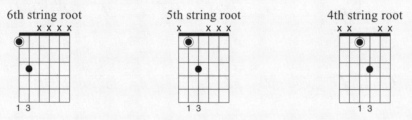

In the "basic moves" below, play all power chords with down strokes. Also play each example using a muted and legato (let ring) approach.

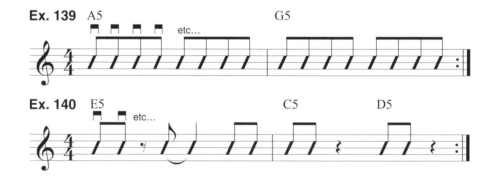

Power Chords with an Added Ninth

Figure 16 shows power chords with the added ninth scale degree. These chords can enhance both major and minor chord types. The written symbol for power chords with the added ninth scale degree is: A5(add9), E5(add9), C5(add9), etc.

Fig. 16: power chords with added ninth

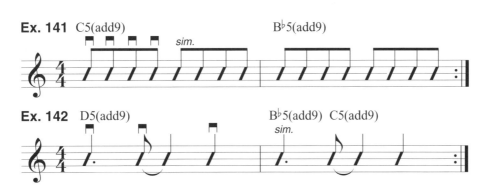

Ex. 141 C5(add9)   *sim.*   B♭5(add9)

Ex. 142 D5(add9)   *sim.*   B♭5(add9) C5(add9)

Chart Reading with Two Parts

The following charts contain two rhythm guitar parts. Use full-voiced barre chords for Gtr. 1 and power chords for Gtr. 2. Your goal here is to play both parts the first time through without mistakes. Make sure to check the chart for repeat signs, multiple endings, coda signs, etc.

Chart #1

Ex. 143

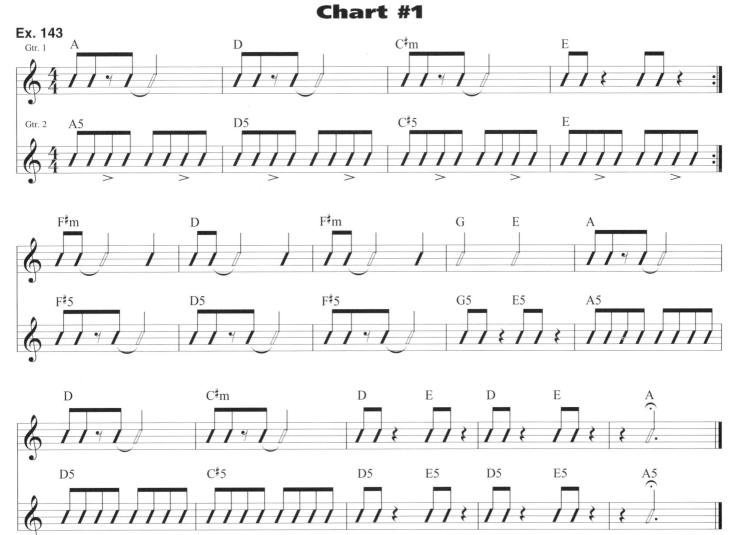

Chart #2

Ex. 143

Notes:

Chapter Seven

7

Objectives

- To learn major and minor 7th chord shapes in open position.
- To learn movable shapes of major and minor 7th chords.
- To play "basic moves"
- To play rhythm charts using given chord types.

This chapter will focus on learning major and minor 7ths in open position as well as some movable shapes with roots on the fifth and sixth strings, since a true open position voicing of some of these chords types is not possible. We will study more of moveable 7th shapes in later chapters.

Open Position Major 7th Chords

Learn the major 7th chord shapes below and practice them in the "basic moves" that follow in exercises 145-147.

Fig. 17: open position major 7th chords

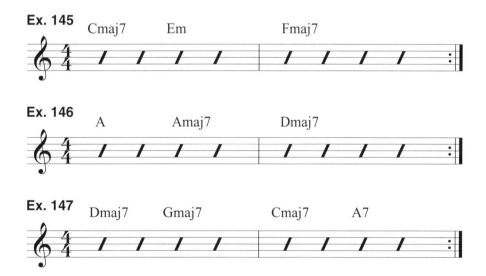

Ex. 145   Cmaj7   Em   Fmaj7

Ex. 146   A   Amaj7   Dmaj7

Ex. 147   Dmaj7   Gmaj7   Cmaj7   A7

Open Position Minor 7th Chords

Learn the minor 7th chord shapes below and practice them in the following "basic moves."

Fig. 18: open position minor 7th chords

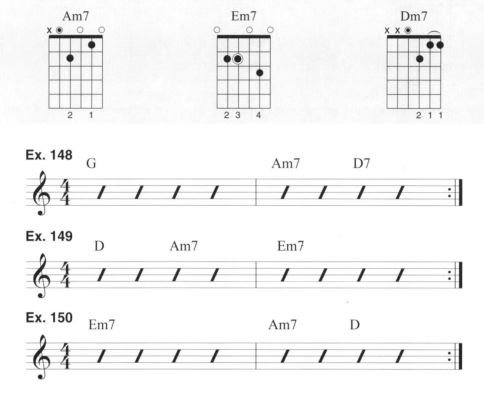

Ex. 148

Ex. 149

Ex. 150

Movable Major 7th Chords

Learn these moveable major 7th chord shapes and use them to play the following "basic moves".

Fig. 19: moveable major 7th shapes, with sixth and fifth string roots

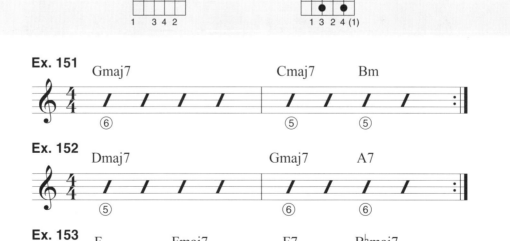

Ex. 151

Ex. 152

Ex. 153

Movable Minor 7th Chords

Learn these moveable minor 7th shapes and use them to play the "basic moves" below.

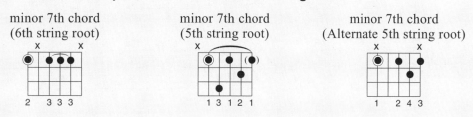

Fig. 20: moveable minor 7th shapes, with sixth and fifth string roots

minor 7th chord (6th string root)

minor 7th chord (5th string root)

minor 7th chord (Alternate 5th string root)

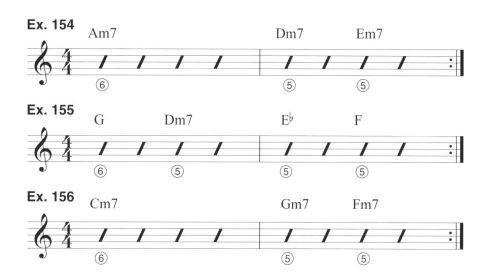

Ex. 154

Ex. 155

Ex. 156

Chart #1

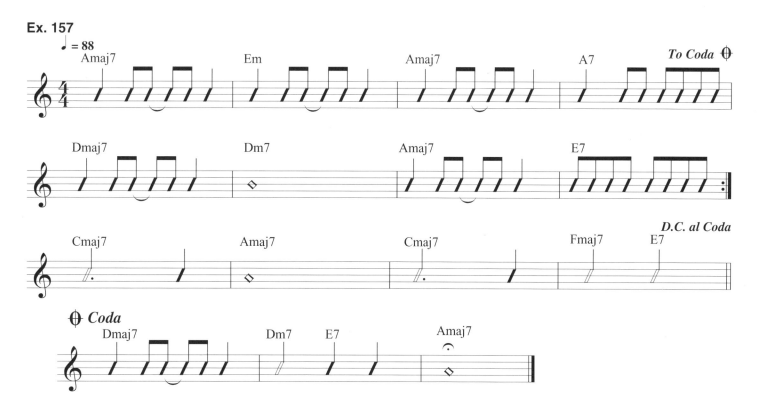

Ex. 157

Chart #2

Ex. 158

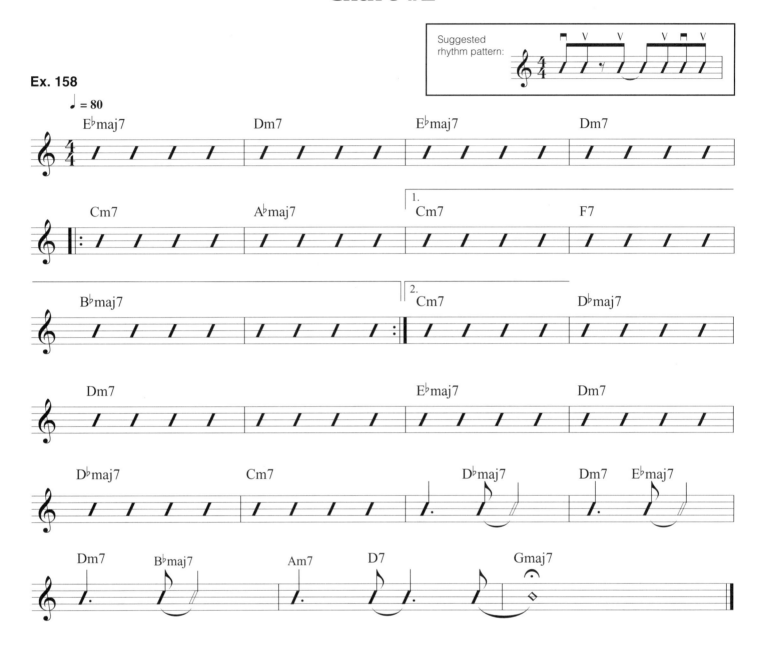

Notes:

Chapter Eight

Objectives

- To learn 6th and dominant 9th chord shapes and their application to blues progressions.
- To play "basic moves."
- To play two-part rhythm charts

This chapter explores 6th and dominant 9th chord shapes in relation to their use in blues progressions. While these two chord sounds work in much more than blues, we will confine their use to blues applications for this chapter. Over most blues progressions, these chord types will work well to create your own part. The trick lies in playing the right chord *voicing* (the specific arrnagement of the notes in the chord) and in understanding how these shapes can be applied over any given harmonic structure.

6th Chords

A 6th chord is a major chord in which the 7th has been replaced with a *6th.* Learn the 6th chord shapes below and use them in the "basic moves" that follow in exercises 159-161. For application, it is not always necessary to play the low root note, so it is shown in parenthesis.

Fig.21: 6th chords, with sixth and fifth string roots

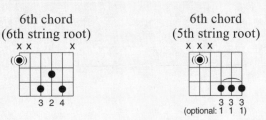

Play the following examples using only the upper three notes and omitting the low root.

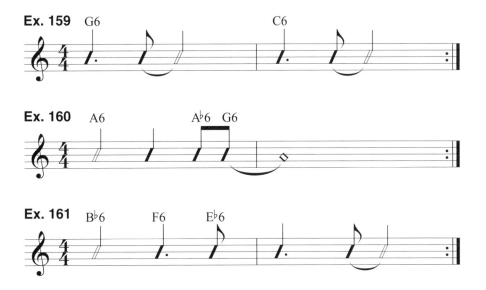

Dominant 9th Chords

Dominant 9th chords consist of a dominant 7th chord plus a 9th tone. Learn the movable shapes below and use them to play the "basic moves" that follow. Again, the low root is optional.

Fig. 22: dominant 9th chords, with sixth and fifth string roots

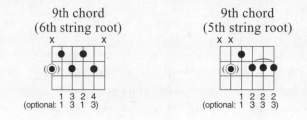

Ex. 162

Ex. 163

Ex. 164

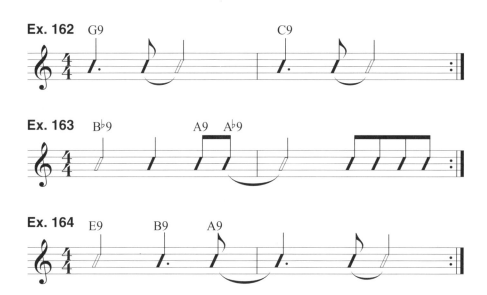

Blues Charts

The following blues charts should be played with both a *straight eighth* note feel and a *shuffle* feel.

Chart #1 is a twelve-bar blues with Gtr. 2 holding up the bottom end while Gtr. 1 plays 6th and dominant 9th embellishments.

Chart #2 is an eight-bar blues with the same format. While most of us know the twelve-bar blues form well, the eight-bar blues form should also be committed to memory.

Finally, write your own twelve-bar blues using the 6th and dominant 9th sounds with your own rhythms over another guitar part like the one used in charts 1 and 2.

Chart #1

"12-bar blues"

Ex. 165

Chart #2

"8-bar blues"

Ex. 166

Write your own!

Notes:

Chapter Nine

Objectives

- To learn more 6th and dominant 9th chord shapes.
- To play "Basic Moves."
- To play rhythm progressions using given chord shapes.

In Chapter 8, we learned some select voicings of 6th and dominant 9th chords to use with blues progressions. In this chapter, we will continue to learn and play more movable shapes of 6th and dominant 9th chord sounds with roots on the sixth, fifth, and fourth strings.

When playing the 6th or dominant 9th voicings, remember the basic underlying chord type has not changed. A C6 chord is still a major type chord and a C9 still contains a dominant 7th chord. The 6th and 9th (or 2nd) scale degrees only enhance and add stylistic color to the basic chord type.

More 6th Chords

Here is another shape for the 6th chord. Use it in the "basic moves" below. (Play all chords with movable shapes.)

Fig. 23: 6th chord, with sixth string root

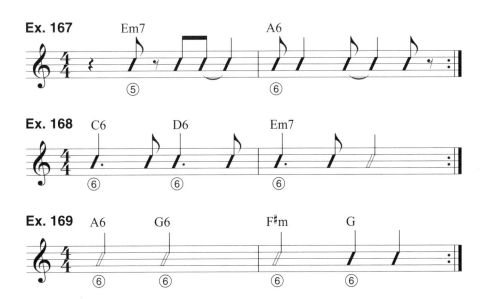

Here are two more 6th chord shapes, with the root on the fifth string. Use these in the "basic moves" below. (Play all other chords with movable shapes with roots on the fifth and sixth strings.)

Fig. 24: 6th chords, with fifth string roots

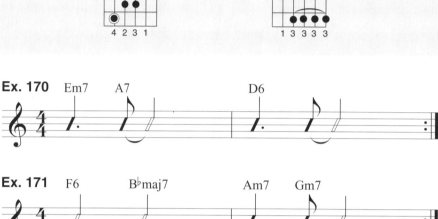

The next 6th chord shape is rooted on the fourth string. Use this movable shape in the "basic moves" that follow.

Fig. 25: 6th chord, with fourth string root

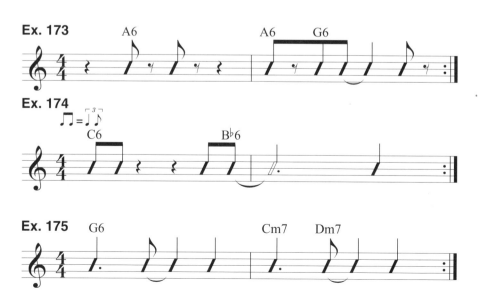

More Dominant 9th Chords

Learn the movable dominant 9th chord shape with roots on the sixth and first string, then practice it in the "basic moves" below. (Play all other chords with movable shapes.)

Fig. 26: 9th chord, with sixth/first string root

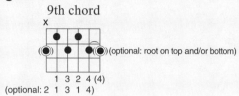

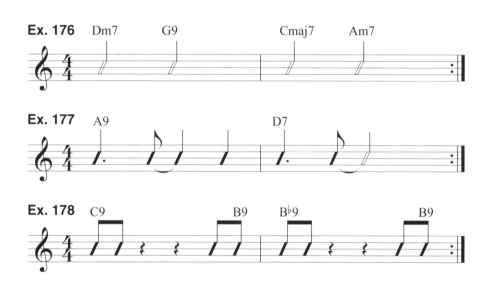

Here are two fingerings for the movable 9th chord shape with fifth string root. Use them in the "basic moves" that follow. (Play all other chords with movable shapes.)

Fig. 27: 9th chords, with fifth string roots

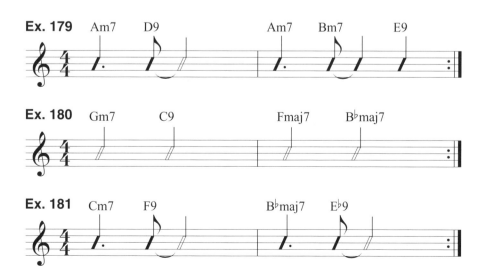

Here is the movable 9th chord shape with fourth string root. Use it in the "basic moves" that follow. (Play all other chords with movable shapes.)

Fig. 28: 9th chord, with fourth string root

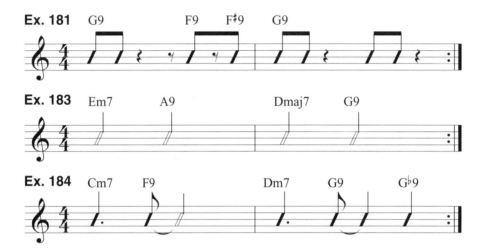

Charts

The following charts are to be played using the indicated voicings. The diagrams are there to help you remember the new shapes and also to give specific voicings to be played. You should memorize these combinations of voicings and see them as "good voice leading." Use these chords together in other songs and progressions. After you can play these combinations, you should then make up some other combinations by starting with the first chord in a different position/voicing and then trying to find the next chord by staying relatively close to the first chord. The more combinations you learn, the greater variety and ease in playing will result.

Finally, it should be stressed that these 6th and 9th chords are among the most common of chords . All shapes should be learned and played regularly. You will eventually hear these voicings and recognize their importance.

Chart #1

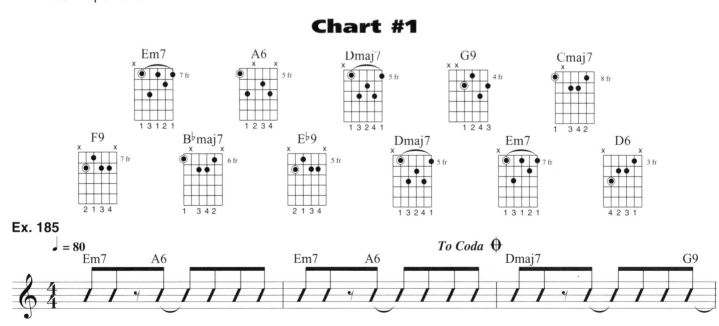

Ex. 185

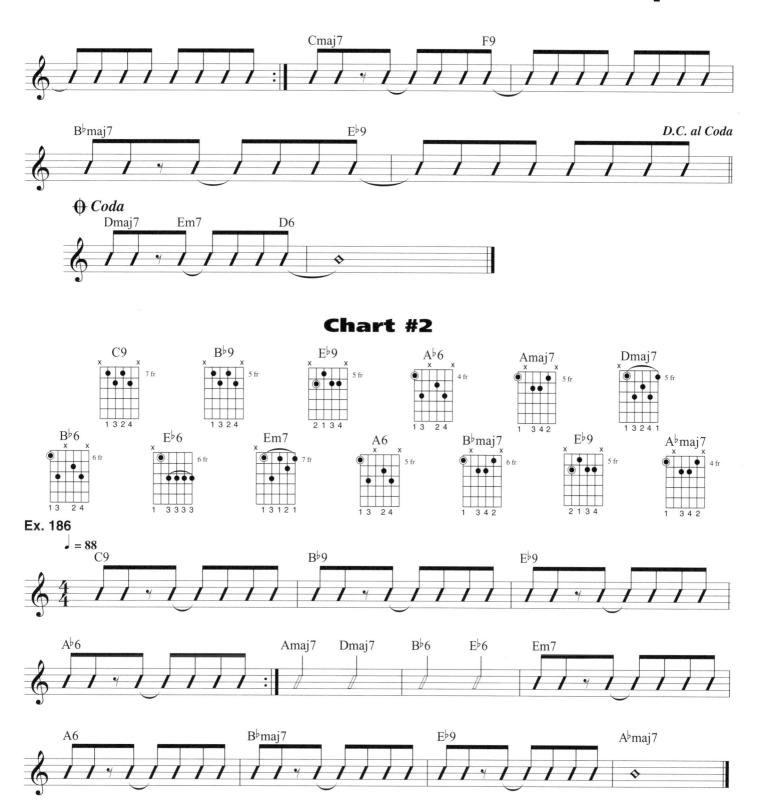

Chart #2

Ex. 186

Notes:

Chapter Ten

Objectives

- To learn the harmonized major scale in triads on the three strings.
- To play "basic moves" using triad shapes.
- To learn Roman Numeral use in harmonized major scales and chord progressions.

The process of building chords on the degrees of the major scale, using only the pitches found within the scale, is called *harmonizing* the scale. In this chapter, we will focus on learning chords from the harmonized major scale in triad shapes on the top three strings only. Knowing three-string triad shapes on the various string sets (1-2-3, 2-3-4, etc.) is essential to good fingerboard knowledge. These shapes are also essential for making up your own part within a larger musical setting, when a chord containing five or six notes might be inappropriate.

Harmonized Major Scale

Figure 29 shows the triads found in the harmonized B♭ major scale. The lowest note of each chord is the root.

Fig. 29: triads in the key of B♭

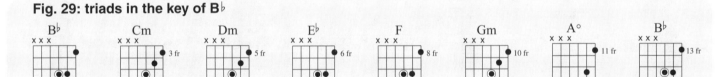

Play the B♭ harmonized major scale below using the shapes from figure 29; ascending and descending, in steady half notes. (The symbol "°" denotes a diminished chord.)

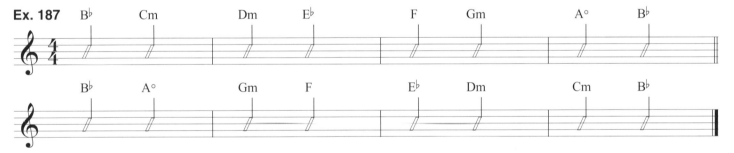

Now play the B♭ harmonized scale in diatonic 3rds, ascending and descending.

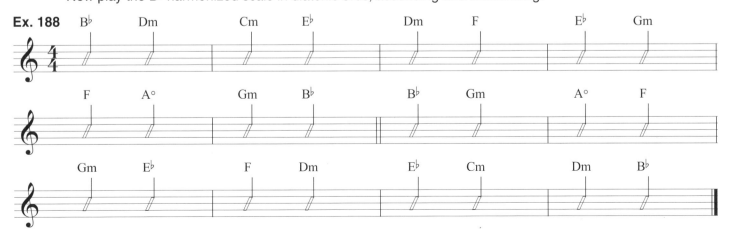

"Basic Moves"

All of the triad shapes learned in figure 29 are movable, so you should play the harmonized scale in all keys. Only in this way will you fully extend your knowledge. In certain keys, chord sequences from the scale may become too high on the fingerboard to play. Simply drop these chord shapes down one octave on the fingerboard and finish playing the scale.

Play the following "basic moves" using the previous three-string triad shapes. Depending on the key you are in, and what chord you are playing next, it is sometimes better to move down to the new chord, since it may be much closer to the present chord you are playing. Look at each example below and decide what direction (up or down) you will move when playing a new chord.

NOTE: Remember, all roots are on the third string. You can use the octave shape starting from the *fifth string* root (shown above, right) to locate the third string root.

octave shape from
5th string to 3rd string:

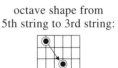

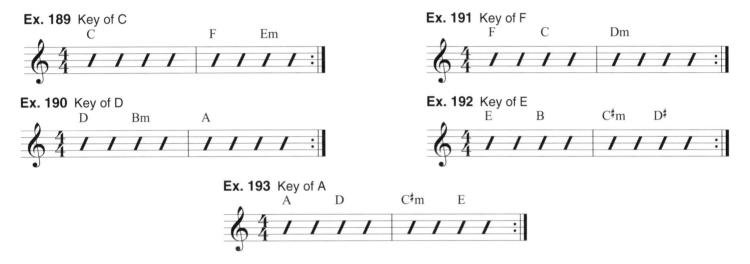

Roman Numeral use in Harmonized Scales and Progressions

We can apply the major scale harmonies we have learned to each scale degree, using the necessary chord type found within the harmonized scale and Roman Numerals to represent them.

Fig. 30: Roman Numerals in key of B♭

Key of B♭							
Chord:	B♭	Cm	Dm	E♭	F	Gm	A°
Roman Numeral:	I	ii	iii	IV	V	vi	vii°

Fill in the correct Roman Numerals in the following chord progressions below and then play them using the three-string triad shapes. Note: Chords I, IV, V are major; chords ii, iii, vi are minor; chord vii° is diminished.

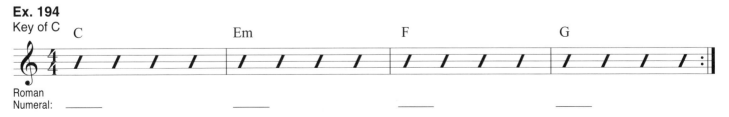

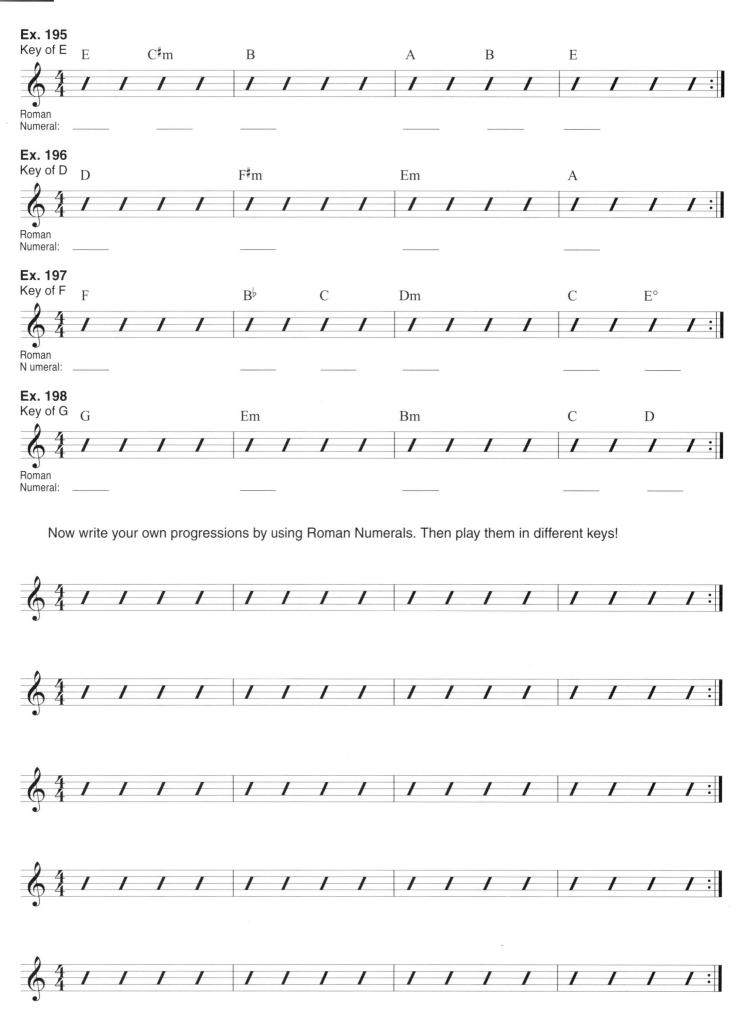

Now write your own progressions by using Roman Numerals. Then play them in different keys!

Chapter Eleven

Objectives

- To analyze and play Roman Numeral chord progressions.
- To play two-part rhythmic chord charts.

Analyzing Roman Numeral Chord Progressions

Write in the chord names for the following Roman Numeral chord progressions in the keys indicated, play them using both full fifth and sixth string root chords (i.e., barre and open position chords). Finally, play each using the three-string triad shapes learned in the last chapter. Use a steady eighth note rhythm.

Ex. 199

Key of C

Key of F

I   vi   ii   V

Ex. 200

Key of D

Key of A

I   IV   V   vi   V

Ex. 201

Key of G

Key of B♭

I   V   vi   IV   iii

Chord Charts

In the chord charts that follow, play part 1 using three-string triads only. Part 2 is a steady eighth note feel using full fifth and sixth string root chords and/or power chords. Play each chart and trade parts.

Chart #1

Ex. 202

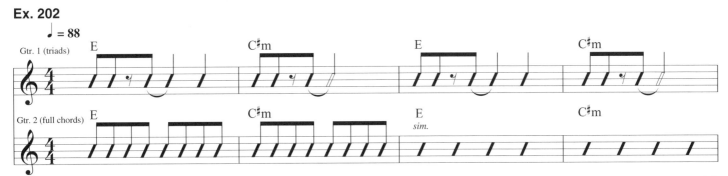

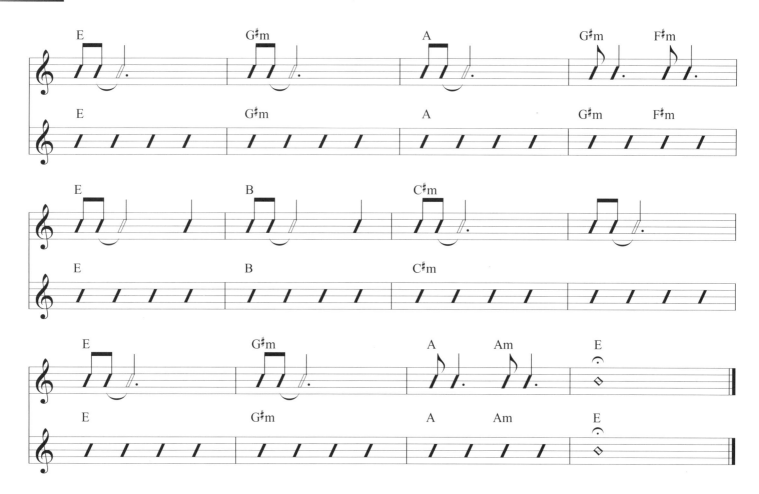

Chart #2

Ex. 203

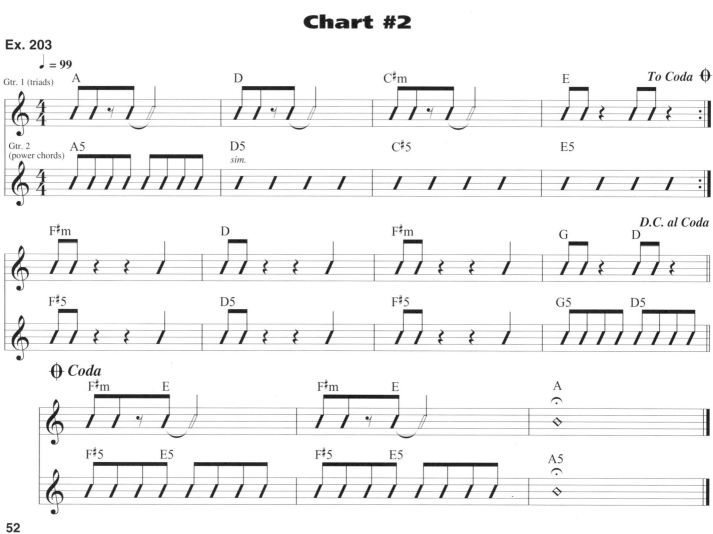

Chapter Twelve

Objectives

- To begin working with sixteenth note rhythms.
- To play chord "vamps" using sixteenth note patterns.
- To learn movable shapes for suspended (sus) 4th and dominant 7sus4 chords.
- To play "basic moves."

Part of the focus of this chapter is to begin playing sixteenth note rhythm patterns, concentrating on the strumming hand. The main idea is to achieve a relaxed, even strum. Practicing with a metronome or drum machine is essential! As you play through each pattern, practice them at slower as well as faster tempos. This will greatly improve your sense of time and feel.

Sixteenth Notes

Let's begin by playing the following sixteenth note rhythms while muting the strings with the fretting hand. Play each example at the following tempos: ♩ = 60 and ♩ = 80. Pay close attention to strumming direction and concentrate on keeping a relaxed feel in your strumming hand as you play. NOTE: *Never look directly at the sun while playing your guitar!*

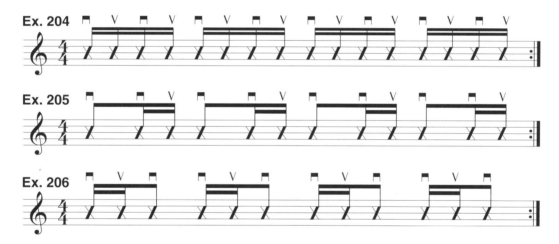

Now let's use chordal attacks and combine some of the rhythms just practiced. Again, pay attention to strumming directions. To develop your rhythmic independence, you should practice on counting the quarter-note pulse out loud, while playing these sixteenth note patterns.

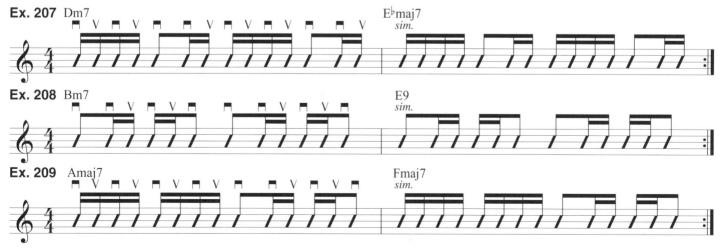

Later, in Chapter 13, we will combine both muted and chordal attacks along with new combinations of sixteenth note patterns. So keep working on the patterns shown on the previous page using your own chord sounds to master these rhythms well.

Suspended 4th Chords

Since suspended 4th chords do not contain a major or minor 3rd, they are generally symbolized only as "sus4." A chord type (major or minor) is not given. However, in theory a sus4 chord that resolves to a major sound is thought of as a "major sus4" while a sus4 chord that resolves to a minor sound is thought of as a "minor sus4."

Fig.31: movable sus4 chord shapes

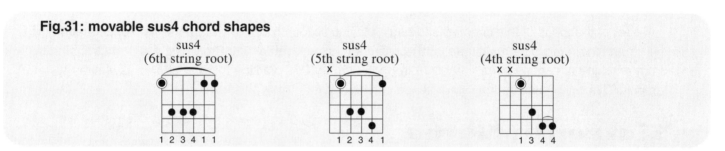

Use sus4 chord in the "basic moves" below.

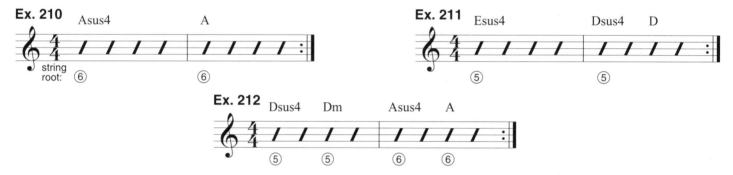

Dominant 7sus4

Although the dominant 7th suspended chord does not contain a major or minor 3rd, it is symbolized as "7sus4" since it does contain a lowered seventh degree. Use these 7sus4 shapes in the "basic moves" below.

Fig. 32: movable 7sus4 chords

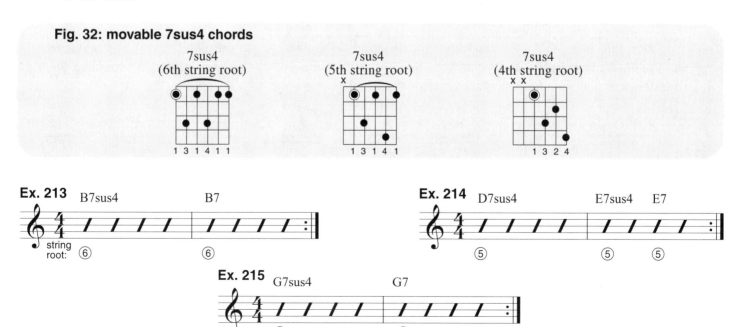

Chapter Thirteen

Objectives

- To learn new sixteenth note rhythms.
- To combine sixteenth note rhythms to play single-measure funk patterns.
- To play charts using new patterns.

In the last chapter, we began learning some sixteenth note rhythms which we combined into short patterns. Let's continue this by adding three new sixteenth note rhythms which we will use in one measure patterns. Remember to always use a metronome or drum machine when practicing these rhythms and play them at different tempos. Suggested tempos for example one are: ♩ = 60 and ♩ = 80.

More Sixteenth Note Figures

Be sure to pay close attention to strumming directions on each rhythm. Use any chord.

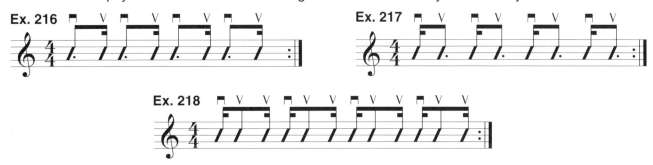

Both the eighth and dotted eighth rhythms in the figures above can be played as sixteenth note "scratch" patterns as in the examples below. Play each example using both interpretations and notice that the chordal attack of each rhythm is the same. Use any chord.

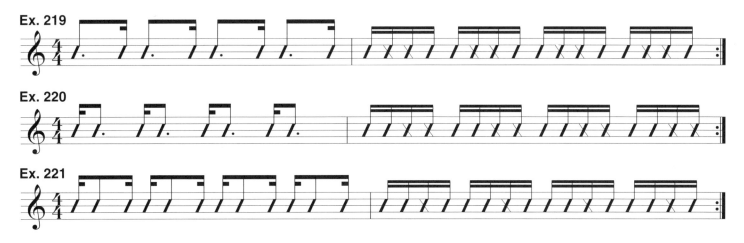

Use the boxes below to write out several chord pairs to use in practicing the rhythms above.

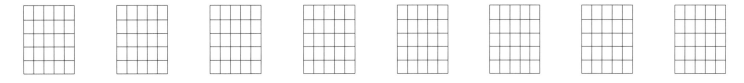

One Measure Patterns

Let's now take some of our sixteenth note rhythms and combine them to make patterns for use in the charts which follow.

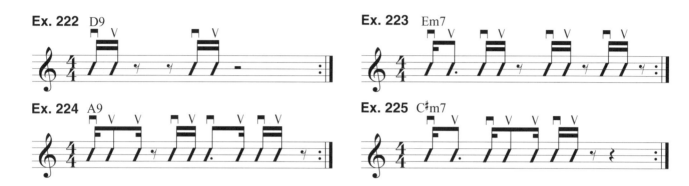

Ex. 222 D9   **Ex. 223** Em7

Ex. 224 A9   **Ex. 225** C#m7

Chart #1

Ex. 226 F9

Chart #2

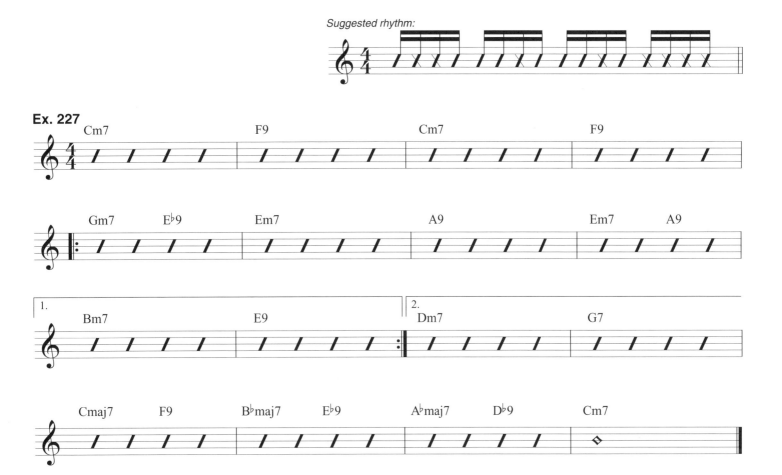

Ex. 227

Notes:

Objectives

- To learn movable shapes of major and minor 9th chords with the root on the sixth and fifth strings.
- To play "basic moves."
- To play rhythm charts using given chords.

Major and Minor 9th Chords

In Chapters 8 and 9 we learned shapes for dominant 9th chords. We will now learn shapes for major and minor 9th chords with the roots on the sixth and fifth strings. When adding a 9th (2nd) to any chord, remember we are not changing the chord type. A major 9th chord is a major 7th chord with the 9th (2nd scale degree) added. A minor 9th chord is a minor 7th chord with the 9th (2nd scale degree) added. The 9th (2nd) scale degree only adds "color" and enhances the existing chord type.

Fig. 33: movable major 9th shapes

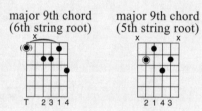

Play the following "basic moves" using the major 9th shapes above.

Ex. 228   Gm7   C9   Fmaj9   string roots: ⑥ ⑤ ⑥

Ex. 229   Dm7   G7   Cmaj9   ⑤ ⑥ ⑤

Ex. 230   Amaj7   C#m7   Dmaj7   Amaj9   ⑥ ⑤ ⑤ ⑥

Ex. 231   Dmaj9 Gmaj7   A7   Bm7   ⑤ ⑥ ⑥ ⑥

Use the minor 9th shapes below in the "basic moves" that follow.

Fig. 34: movable minor 9th shapes

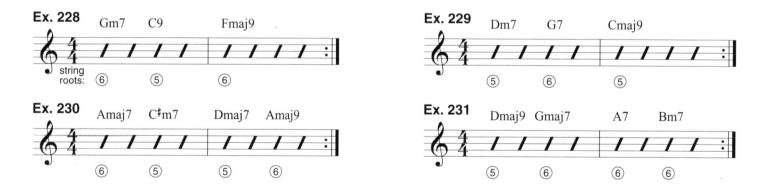

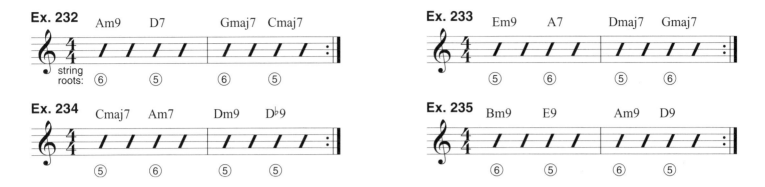

Ex. 232   Am9   D7   Gmaj7 Cmaj7

string roots: ⑥ ⑤ ⑥ ⑤

Ex. 233   Em9   A7   Dmaj7 Gmaj7

⑤ ⑥ ⑤ ⑥

Ex. 234   Cmaj7 Am7   Dm9   D♭9

⑤ ⑥ ⑤ ⑤

Ex. 235   Bm9   E9   Am9   D9

⑥ ⑤ ⑥ ⑤

Charts

The following charts use major and minor 9th chords, as well as dominant 9th chord. Choose a set of chord shapes and write them in the diagrams below each chart.

Chart #1

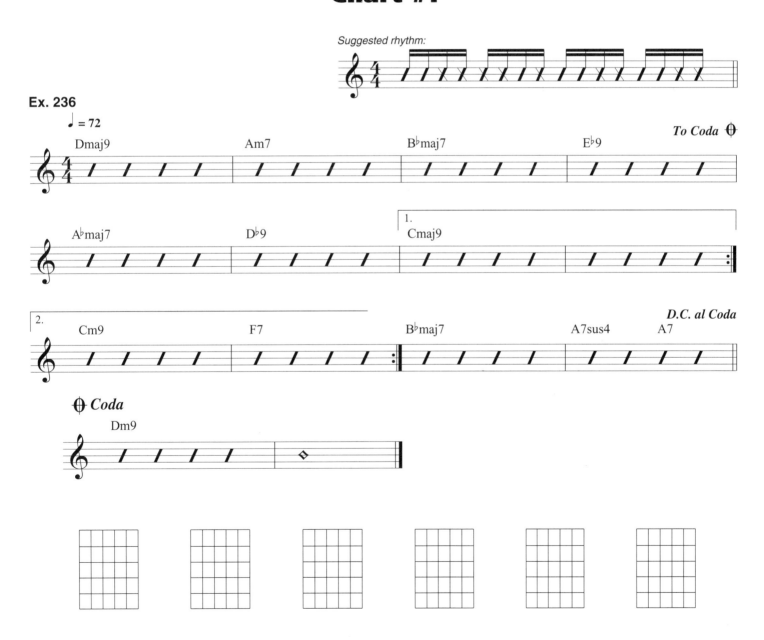

Suggested rhythm:

Ex. 236

♩ = 72

To Coda ⊕

Dmaj9   Am7   B♭maj7   E♭9

A♭maj7   D♭9   1. Cmaj9

D.C. al Coda

2. Cm9   F7   B♭maj7   A7sus4 A7

⊕ *Coda*

Dm9

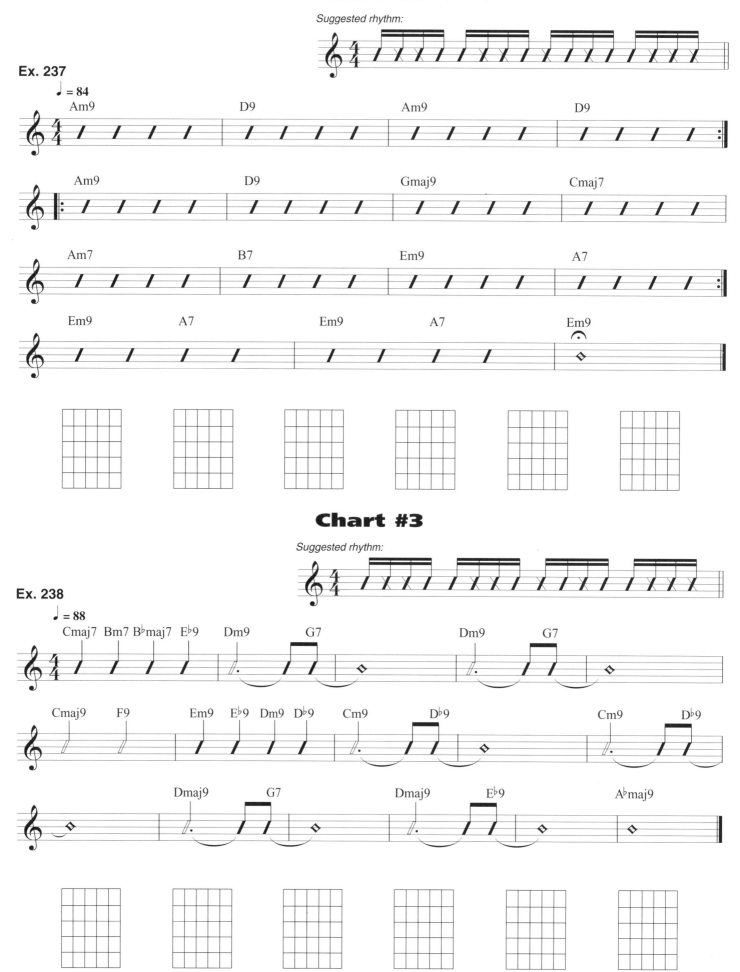

Chapter Fifteen

Objectives

- To learn shapes for minor 7th flat five chords with roots on the sixth and fifth strings.
- To play "basic moves."
- To play rhythmic charts using given chords.

Minor 7♭5

The minor 7♭5 chord type is an important one because of its relationship to other chord types (i.e., dominant 9th, minor 6th, "slash" chords). Depending on its function, it can be called several different names. Although it functions as a chord in the harmonized major scale, its most common usage is found as a ii chord in minor keys.

Fig. 35: movable minor 7♭5 chords

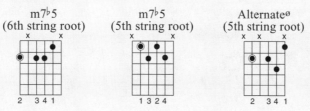

Use the m7♭5 shapes shown above in the "basic moves" below.

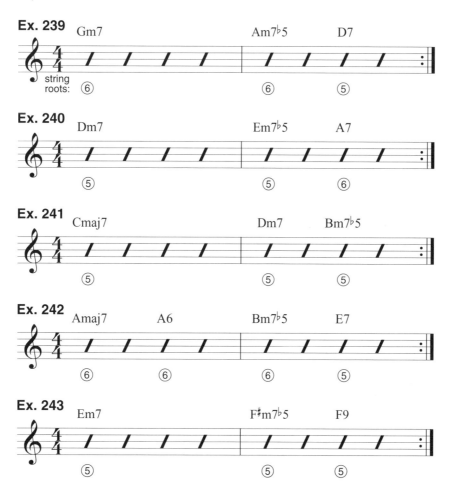

Charts

The following charts also employ m7♭5 chords.

Chart #1

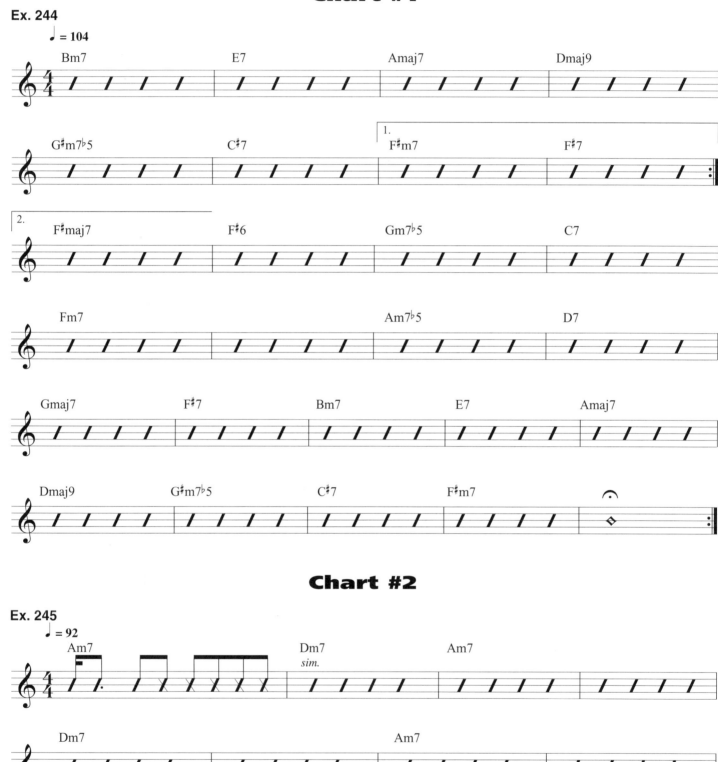

Ex. 244

♩ = 104

Bm7 | E7 | Amaj7 | Dmaj9

G♯m7♭5 | C♯7 | 1. F♯m7 | F♯7

2. F♯maj7 | F♯6 | Gm7♭5 | C7

Fm7 | Am7♭5 | D7

Gmaj7 | F♯7 | Bm7 | E7 | Amaj7

Dmaj9 | G♯m7♭5 | C♯7 | F♯m7

Chart #2

Ex. 245

♩ = 92

Am7 | Dm7 Am7
sim.

Dm7 | Am7

Fmaj7 | Bm7♭5 E7 | Am7 Am9

Chart #3

Ex. 246

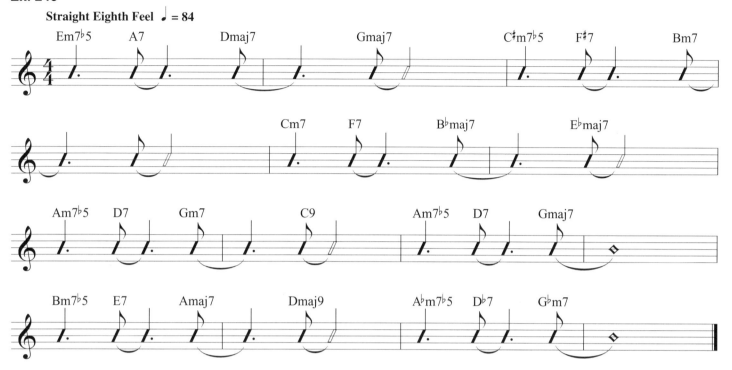

Notes:

Chapter Sixteen
16

Objectives

- To learn shapes for minor 11th chords with roots on the sixth and fifth strings.
- To learn shapes for dominant 9th sus4 chords with roots on the sixth and fifth strings.
- To play "basic moves"
- To play rhythmic charts using given chords.

In this chapter, we continue to look at extended chords, learning the minor 11th and dominant 9sus4 shapes. As we saw previously, the 9th is actually the 2nd scale step. Using this same principal, the 11th is the same as the 4th step of the scale.

11th and 9sus4 Chords

Since any chord containing a major 3rd or major 7th is considered to sound too harsh with the addition of the natural 11th, we will look at only the *minor 11th* chord type along with the *dominant 9sus4* chord type. Remember that the 4th (11th) is acceptable in the dominant 9sus4 because there is no major 3rd. Since no major 3rd appears in the chord, we call it "sus 4" rather than 11th!

Note: However, it is common to see a dominant 9sus4 chord called (incorrectly) a "dominant 11th." For instance, "A9sus4" may sometimes be seen as "A11." The dominant 9sus4 is also commonly known as a "slash" chord, (A9sus4 = G/A). Stay tuned for more slash chords and their function in later chapters. In this chapter we will label the chord only as a "9sus4".

Fig. 36: minor 11th chords

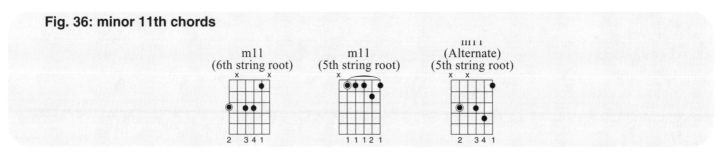

The following "basic moves" use minor 11th chords.

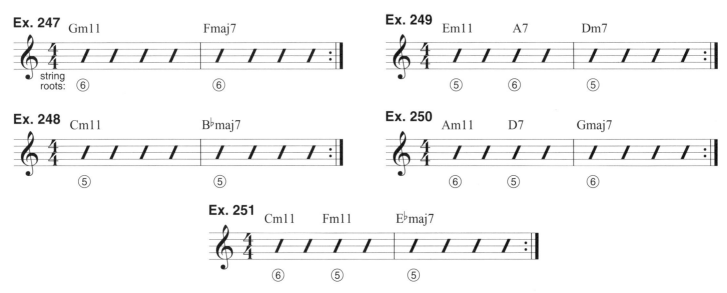

Ex. 247   Gm11   Fmaj7
string roots: ⑥   ⑥

Ex. 248   Cm11   B♭maj7
⑤   ⑤

Ex. 249   Em11   A7   Dm7
⑤   ⑥   ⑤

Ex. 250   Am11   D7   Gmaj7
⑥   ⑤   ⑥

Ex. 251   Cm11   Fm11   E♭maj7
⑥   ⑤   ⑤

Fig. 37: dominant 9sus4 chords

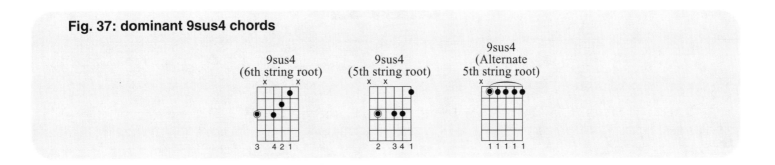

The following "basic moves" include 9sus4 chords.

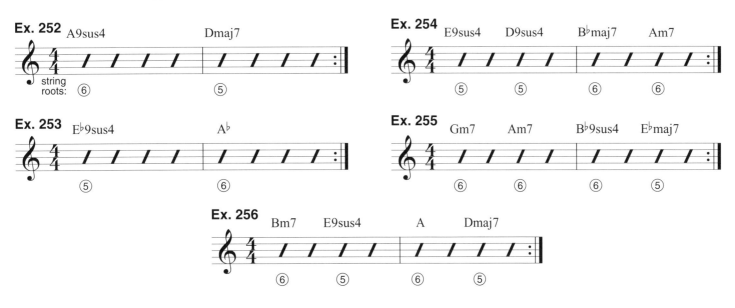

Charts

The following charts incorporate m11 and 9sus4 chords. In Chart #1, notice the half-step motion in the bass with different chord types. Observe where any common tones appear in the chords.

Chart #1

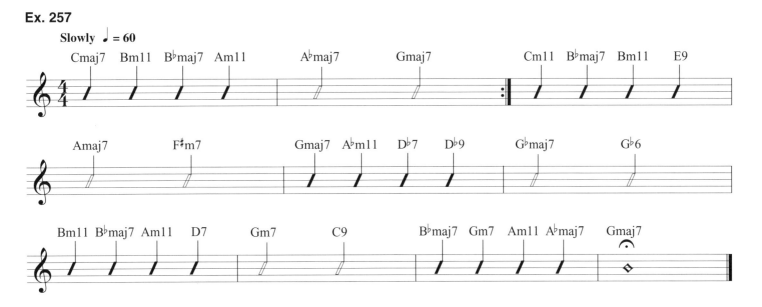

Chart #2

Suggested rhythm:

Ex. 258

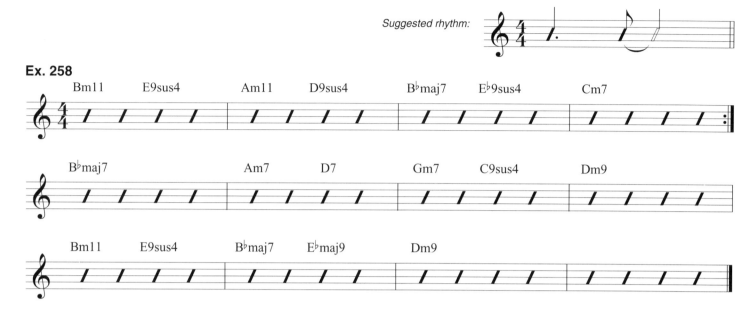

Chart #3

Ex. 259

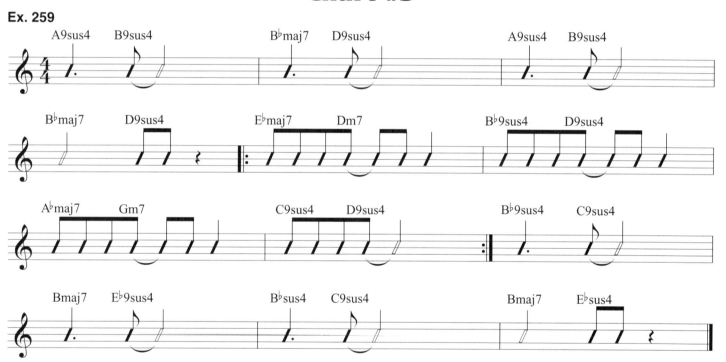

Notes:

Chapter Seventeen

17

Objectives

- To learn major 7th and minor 7th chord shapes with roots on the fourth string.
- To play "basic moves."
- To play rhythm charts using given chords.

Up to this point, we have learned and played most chord shapes with the roots on the fifth and sixth strings. Now we will begin learning some shapes with roots on the fourth string and combine them with other chords learned previously. One advantage to using chords with root on the fourth string is it allows us to have less movement between chord changes. In fact, you may stay in one position to play most chord progressions if desired.

Major and Minor 7ths with Fourth String Root

Two shapes are shown for each major 7th and minor 7th chord. While the first shape given is more practical, (the second shape of the minor 7th is a stretch!) work on both and apply them to chord progressions you already know.

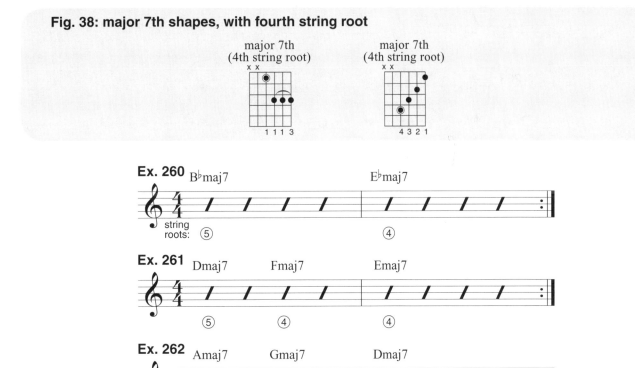

Fig. 38: major 7th shapes, with fourth string root

Fig. 39: minor 7th shapes, with fourth string root

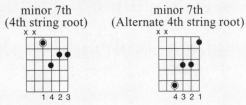

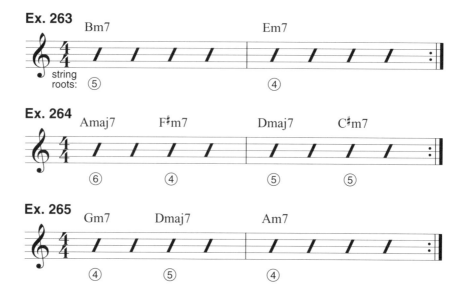

"Basic Moves"

These "basic moves" combine both major and minor 7ths with fourth string roots.

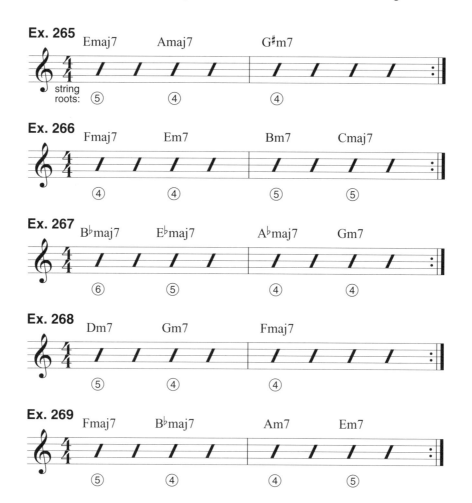

Charts

Chart #1 mixes fourth-string-root 7th chords together with fifth- and sixth-root 7ths. In chart #2, play all voicings with the root on the fourth string.

Chart #1

Ex. 270

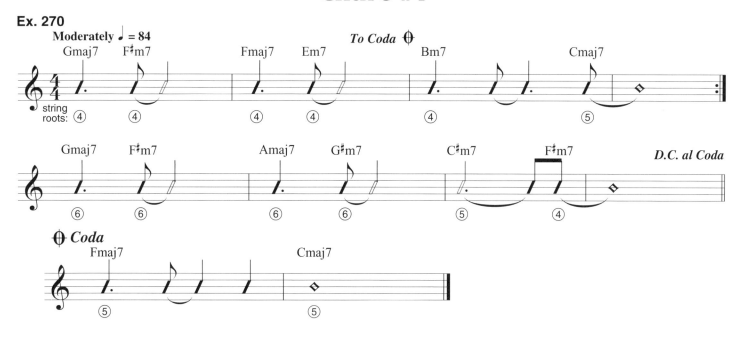

Chart #2

("Dotty Said No")

Ex. 271

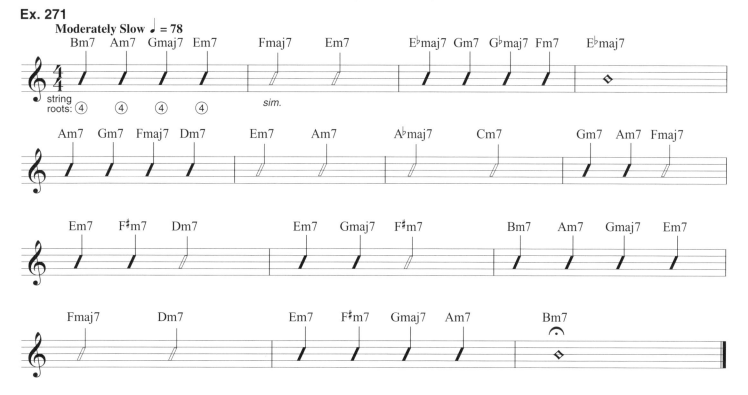

Notes:

Chapter Eighteen

18

Objectives

- To learn dominant 7th and minor 7♭5 chord shapes with roots on the 4th string.
- To play "basic moves."
- To play charts using given chords.

Here we will continue with fourth string root chords by adding the dominant 7th and minor 7♭5. By knowing these four chord types, with the roots on the sixth, fifth, and fourth strings, you are well on your way to playing most chord progressions in one position. (In later chapters, we will explore this in detail.)

Dominant 7th and Minor 7♭5 Chords with Fourth String Roots

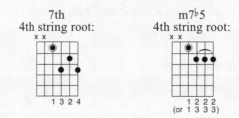

Fig. 40: dominant 7th and minor 7♭5 chords, with fourth string root

The following "basic moves" use dominant 7th chords with fourth string roots, followed by m7♭5 chords with fourth string roots.

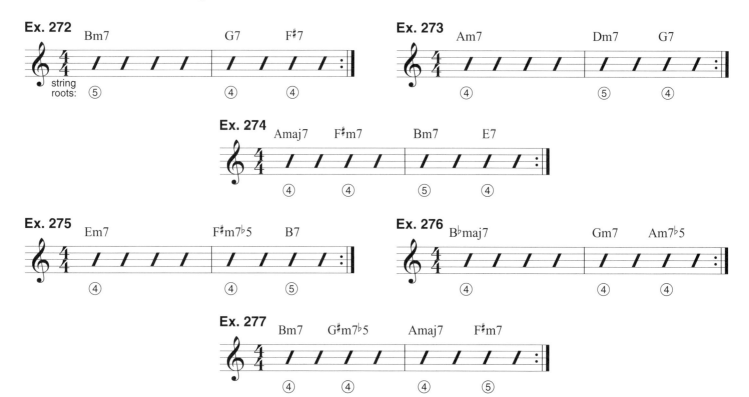

Charts

The following charts mix 7th and m7♭5 chords with fourth string roots.

Chart #1

Ex. 278

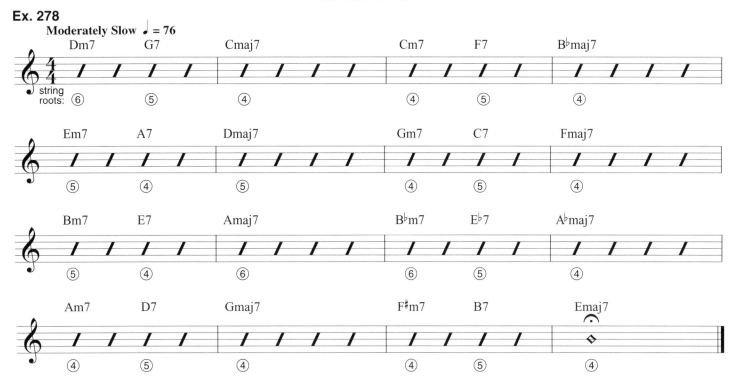

Chart #2

Ex. 279

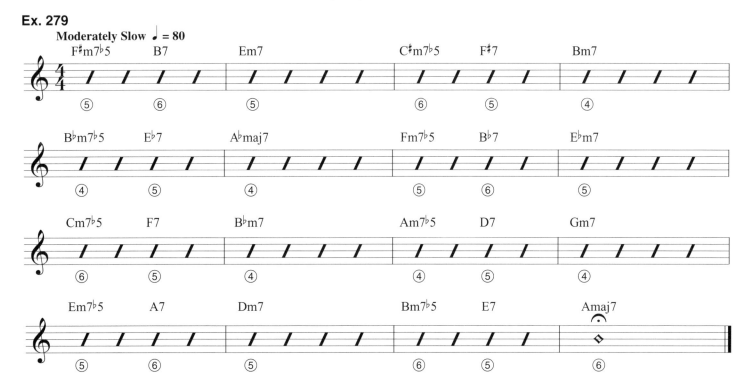

Notes:

Chapter Nineteen

19

Objectives

- To learn the layout of the neck in the "five patterns."
- To learn five patterns for major and minor chords.
- To work on "basic moves."
- To play progressions with rhythms.

The Five Patterns

The five "patterns" on the guitar represent five areas on the fretboard that can be identified by the locations of the roots. Scales are traditionally taught in this manner, but chords are often not. However, it is very important to also view chords in this manner because it helps set up a relationship between chords and scales. Of course there is already a connection between chords and scales through the study of harmony and theory but it is best to also see physical connection on the guitar. The easier it becomes to see the roots related to a position, the easier it is to spot a chord as well as its arpeggio and its scale, all at once. This is a method of practicing and viewing the neck that greatly improves one's ability and combines three essential elements (chord, arpeggio, scale) into one routine that can be maintained as you learn new things. It breaks down the barriers between these three elements that sometimes have a tendency to be separated. Instead, we will see them as different interpretations of the same thing.

Fig. 41: three ways of viewing A7

By practicing in this manner you will be able to access more choices for chord voicings and not be limited to just one or two voicings for a common chord type like major 7th, minor 7th, dominant 7th, etc. Then your choice of which voicing you play will be based more on a *musical* concept rather than a purely physical reason.

Here are the five areas we call patterns, shown with C roots. These patterns are sectioned off by the octave shapes contained within them. Each root is shared between two positions. It is in this way they are connected.

Fig. 42: patterns 1-5 for C

Pattern 2
(roots on 5th and 3rd)

Pattern 4
(roots on 6th, 4th and 1st)

Pattern 1
(roots on 5th and 2nd)

Pattern 3
(roots on 6th, 3rd and 1st)

Pattern 5
(roots on 4th and 2nd)

Once these patterns are linked up, they remain connected in the same way regardless of what note the root happens to be. As you look at different roots, the first pattern will change to another position (fret) on the neck, but all other patterns will remain connected in the same reltationship. The best way to see this is to do the "octave jump" exercise which follows.

"Octave Jump" Exercise

Play the roots of each pattern by "bouncing" back and forth between them in a rhythmic way (keep a steady beat). After staying in one position for a little while and observing the pattern you are in, move up or down to the next pattern. Continue until you have gone through all five positions for one root (C, for example) then switch the root to a new note and go up or down for that root. Do this on at least three roots everyday for three minutes for every practice session for one month. Change the three roots everyday. It is best to always start the exercise from the lowest pattern on the neck for the root you are looking at (i.e., C's lowest pattern is pattern 1, F's lowest pattern is pattern 4).

Let's take a look at the five patterns and the major triads contained therein.

Fig. 43: D major chords and roots, in patterns 1-5

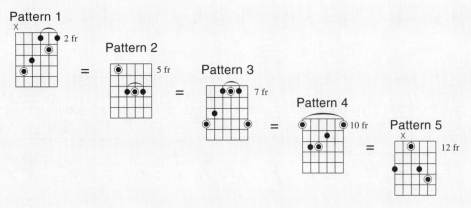

Each diagram starts at the "shared" fret indicated by the equals (=) sign. Notice the *shared root* at the fret indicated! These five patterns show D major. (C major involves open strings in pattern 1 so we raised it to D major.)

Here are the five patterns with their minor triads:

Fig. 44: D minor chords and roots, in patterns 1-5

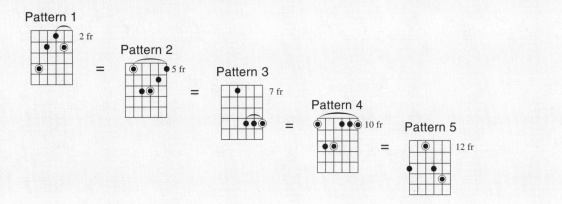

Progressions

As you play the following progressions, choose chord shapes near one another. Use different patterns for each starting chord.

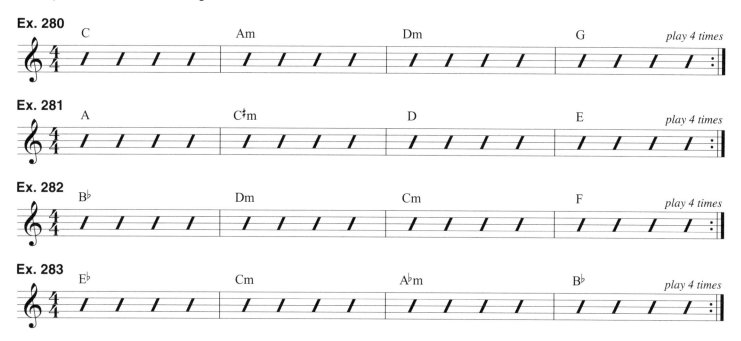

Ex. 280

C   Am   Dm   G   *play 4 times*

Ex. 281

A   C♯m   D   E   *play 4 times*

Ex. 282

B♭   Dm   Cm   F   *play 4 times*

Ex. 283

E♭   Cm   A♭m   B♭   *play 4 times*

As you play the following progressions, switch between two different voicings for each chord.

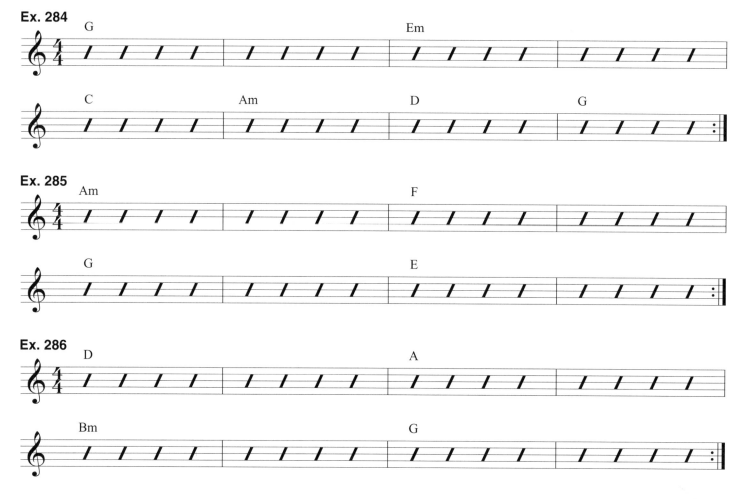

Ex. 284

G   Em

C   Am   D   G

Ex. 285

Am   F

G   E

Ex. 286

D   A

Bm   G

Ex. 287

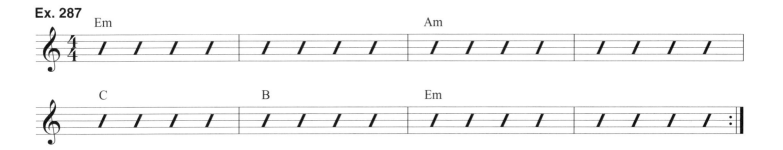

Cycle of Fourths Exercise

The exercise below uses all five patterns with the chords rising through the cycle of fourths. The cycle of fourths (and fifths) should be committed to memory because most songs use this cycle in their chord progressions, and because it will take you through all twelve keys (as does this exercise).

Play through the exercise with a quarter note on each chord. First use only major chord types; next, use only minor chord types; then try a combination of both. The exercise starts on C in pattern 1 (open position) and stops on C in pattern 1 (twelfth position), an octave higher.

Tempo ♩ = 60

Pattern:	1	4	2	5	3	
start here →	C →	F →	B♭ →	E♭ →	A♭	(→)
	D♭	G♭	B (C♭)	E	A	
	D	G	C	F	B♭	
	E♭	A♭	D♭	G♭	B	
	E	A	D	G	C	
	F	B♭	E♭	A♭	D♭	
	G♭	B	E	A	D	
	G	C	F	B♭	E♭	
	A♭	D♭	G♭	B	E	
	A	D	G	C	F	
	B♭	E♭	A♭	D♭	G♭	
	B	E	A	D	G	
	C					

Notes:

Chapter Twenty

Voicing

In this chapter we will continue to work on the five patterns of major and minor triads. By now you may have noticed these chords sound somewhat different even though they are the same letter name and type. This is because they are different *voicings.*

The voicing refers to the order of chord tones *upward* from the bass note.

- One voicing might be: 1, 5, 1, 3, 5, 1.
- Another might be: 3, 1, 5, 1.
- Another might be: 1, 3, 5, 1, 3.

So the *order* in which the chord tones occur has some effect on the sound, but it does not change the basic sound quality. For example, all major chords will sound major, but different voicings will have a somewhat different *shade* of sound.

Here are some variations of the five basic chord shapes for major and minor presented in the last chapter. The smaller shapes extracted from the larger ones are very important because they have a different density of sound and are more appropriate for some situations. Part of having a good rhythm guitar vocabulary is knowing which voicing is correct for the style and instrumentation. Be sure to compare the variations to the original. Most of the time, they are a smaller version of the original shape. Fingerings are left out so that you can focus on the octave shapes. See the root! Experiment with all possible fingerings!

Fig. 45: major shapes and alternate voicings

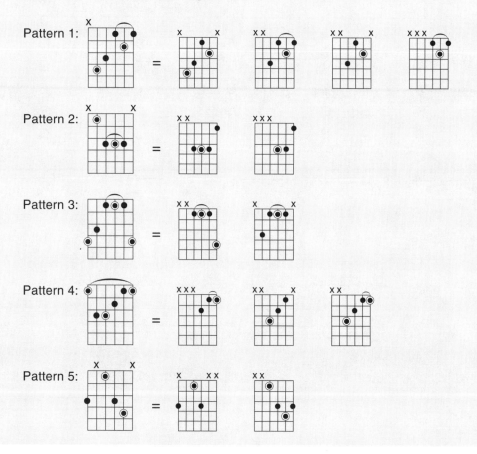

Chapter 21

Fig. 46: minor shapes and alternate voicings

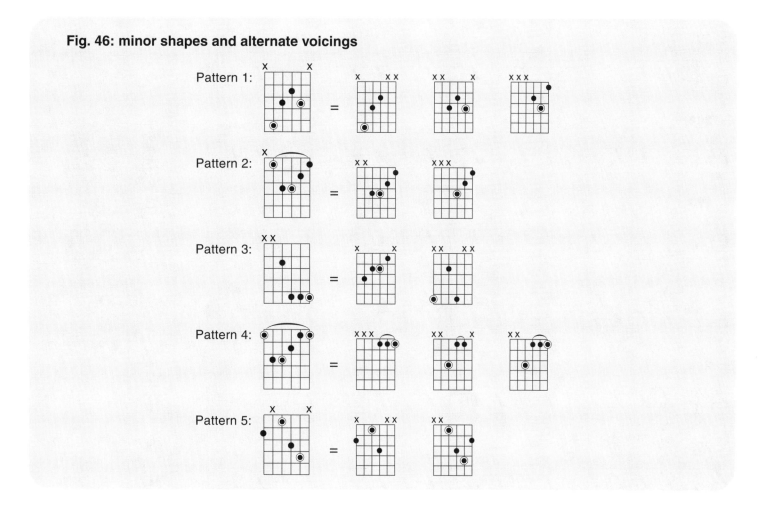

These variations are often inversions of the chord. See which note is in the bass as you learn each shape. The trick to using these smaller shapes is to see them as part of the larger shapes. Put them into some "basic moves" and progressions so you can hear them as a certain type of chord sound. Also see where the root lies in every shape.

"Basic Moves"

Use the smaller shapes shown to the right of each exercise in the following "basic moves." These are meant to not only give you physical practice, but also to give you practice hearing these combinations of chords as "units" of sound. Practice each move in *every* key.

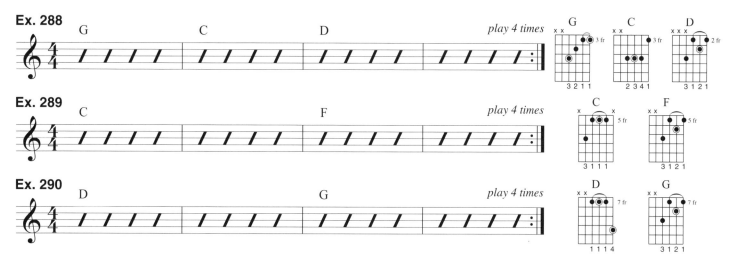

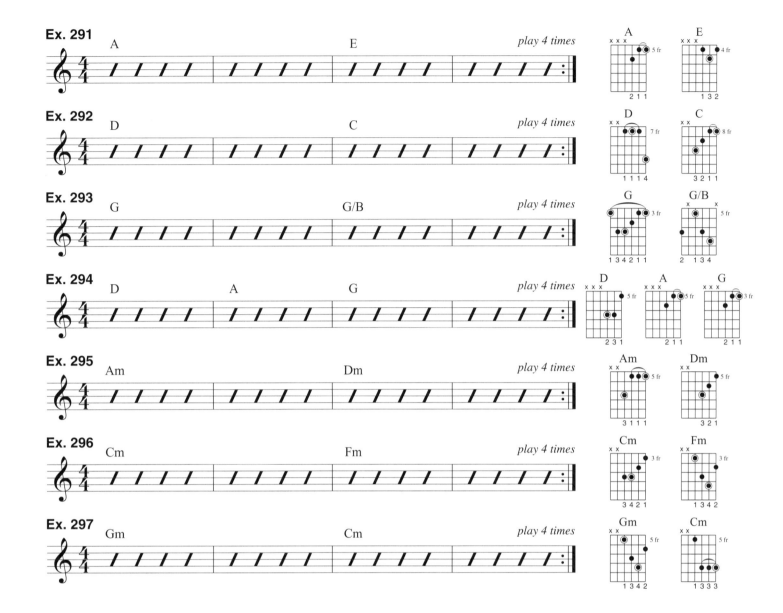

Progressions

Improvise different chord voicings as you play the following progressions. Also, improvise strum patterns for the "hash marks."

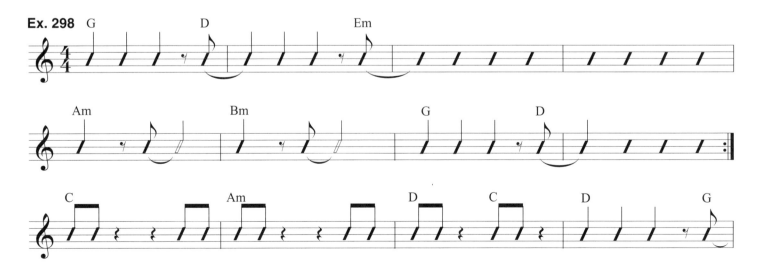

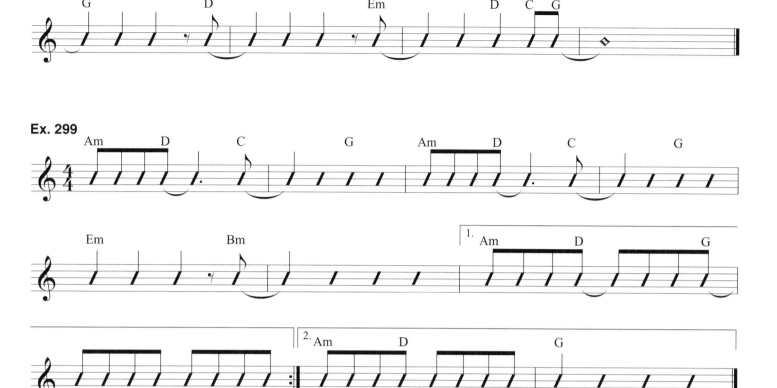

Chapter 20

Ex. 299

Notes:

Chapter Twenty-One

Objectives

- To learn major 7th, minor 7th, and dominant 7th chords built from major scale fingering patterns 1, 2, and 4.
- To play "basic moves."
- To play rhythmic progressions.
- To review five positions of major and minor triads.

In Chapters 6 and 7, we learned and played major and minor triad shapes built from the five major scale fingering patterns. Chapters 8 and 9 will concentrate on major 7th, minor 7th, and dominant 7th chord types, also built from the five major scale fingering patterns. In this section, only patterns 1, 2, and 4 of these chord types are shown.

Formulas for 7th Chords

Seventh chords consist of four notes from the major scale: root, third, fifth, and seventh (1–3–5–7). The breakdown for each chord type is:

- **Major 7th**: The major 7th chord consists of a major triad with an added major 7th interval. The formula is: root, major 3rd, perfect 5th, major 7th, or 1–3–5–7.

- **Dominant 7th**: The dominant 7th chord consists of a major triad with an added minor 7th interval. The formula is: root, major 3rd, perfect 5th, minor 7th, or 1–3–5–♭7.

- **Minor 7th**: The minor 7th chord consists of a minor triad with an added minor 7th interval. The formula is: root, minor 3rd, perfect 5th, minor 7th, or 1–♭3–5–♭7.

Major 7th Chord Shapes

Figure 47 below show the Cmaj7 chords for patterns 1, 2, and 4.

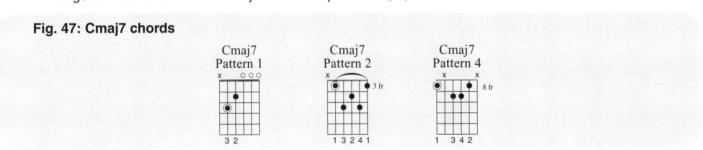

Fig. 47: Cmaj7 chords

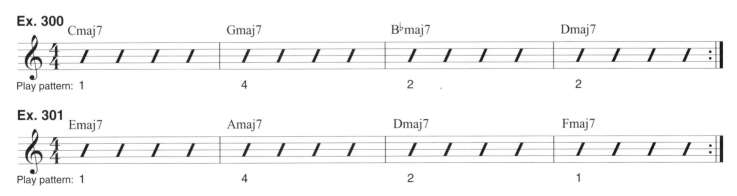

Ex. 300

Cmaj7   Gmaj7   B♭maj7   Dmaj7

Play pattern: 1   4   2   2

Ex. 301

Emaj7   Amaj7   Dmaj7   Fmaj7

Play pattern: 1   4   2   1

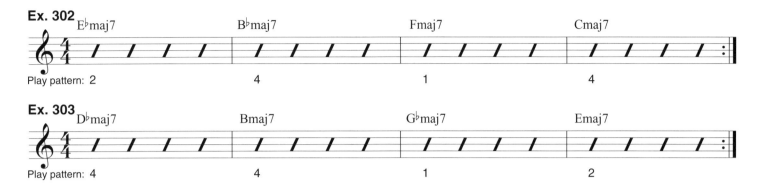

Ex. 302 E♭maj7 ... B♭maj7 ... Fmaj7 ... Cmaj7
Play pattern: 2 ... 4 ... 1 ... 4

Ex. 303 D♭maj7 ... Bmaj7 ... G♭maj7 ... Emaj7
Play pattern: 4 ... 4 ... 1 ... 2

Dominant 7th chord shapes

Figure 48 shows the C7 chords in patterns 1, 2, and 4, plus an alternate pattern 4 shape.

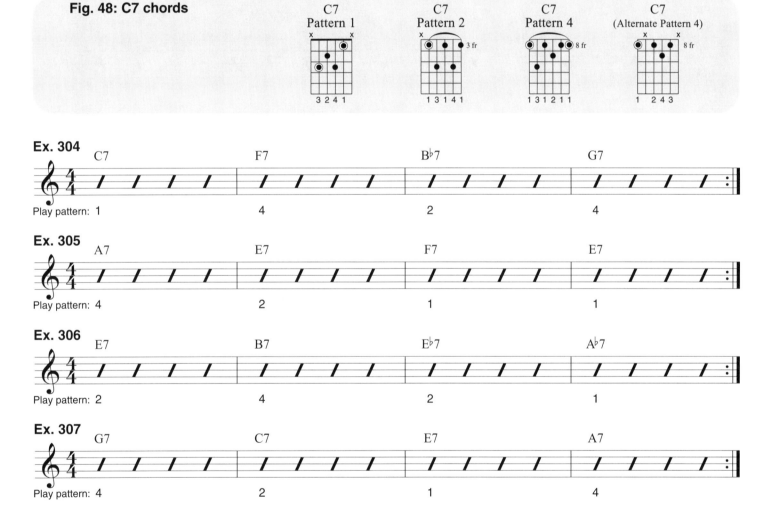

Fig. 48: C7 chords

Ex. 304 C7 ... F7 ... B♭7 ... G7
Play pattern: 1 ... 4 ... 2 ... 4

Ex. 305 A7 ... E7 ... F7 ... E7
Play pattern: 4 ... 2 ... 1 ... 1

Ex. 306 E7 ... B7 ... E♭7 ... A♭7
Play pattern: 2 ... 4 ... 2 ... 1

Ex. 307 G7 ... C7 ... E7 ... A7
Play pattern: 4 ... 2 ... 1 ... 4

Minor 7th Chord Shapes

Figure 49 shows the Cm7 chords in patterns 1, 2, and 4, plus an alternate pattern 2 fingering.

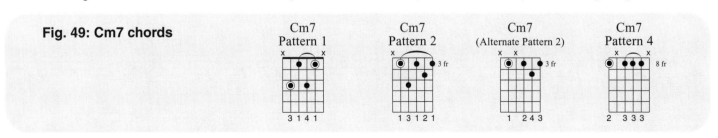

Fig. 49: Cm7 chords

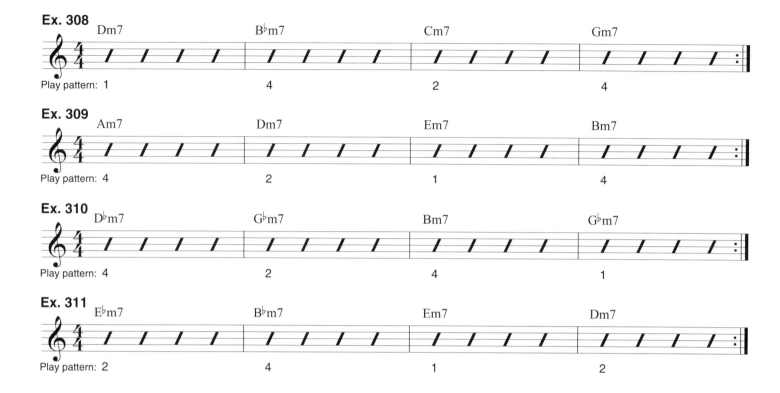

Ex. 308

Dm7   B♭m7   Cm7   Gm7

Play pattern: 1   4   2   4

Ex. 309

Am7   Dm7   Em7   Bm7

Play pattern: 4   2   1   4

Ex. 310

D♭m7   G♭m7   Bm7   G♭m7

Play pattern: 4   2   4   1

Ex. 311

E♭m7   B♭m7   Em7   Dm7

Play pattern: 2   4   1   2

"Basic Moves"

The "basic moves" below all use the major 7th, dominant 7th, and minor 7th chord shapes learned in this chapter. You decide which chord shapes to play, making sure to keep all roots within a six fret range of each other.

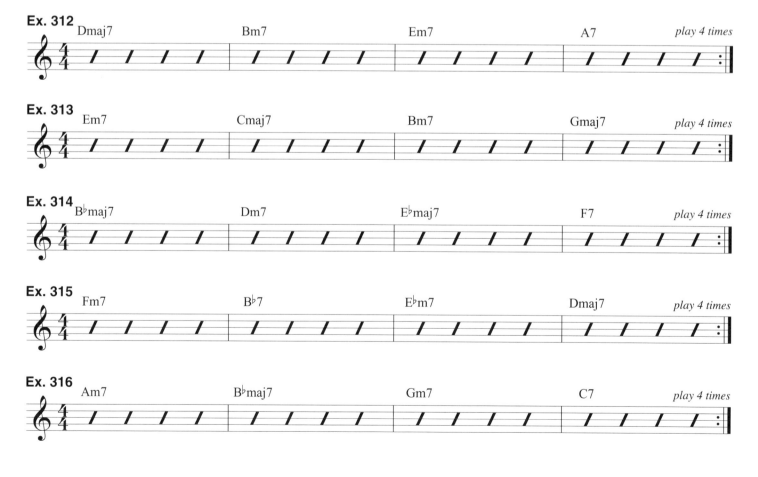

Ex. 312

Dmaj7   Bm7   Em7   A7   *play 4 times*

Ex. 313

Em7   Cmaj7   Bm7   Gmaj7   *play 4 times*

Ex. 314

B♭maj7   Dm7   E♭maj7   F7   *play 4 times*

Ex. 315

Fm7   B♭7   E♭m7   Dmaj7   *play 4 times*

Ex. 316

Am7   B♭maj7   Gm7   C7   *play 4 times*

Progressions

The following progressions use the major 7th, dominant 7th, and minor 7th chord shapes presented in this chapter. As a general rule, remember to keep all chord shapes within a six fret range of each other. Use the suggested rhythm patterns (strums) given with each progression and pay close attention to the repeats, multiple endings, and Codas.

Chapter Twenty-Two

Objectives

- To learn major 7th, minor 7th, and dominant 7th chord shapes built from the major scale in fingering patterns 3 and 5.
- To connect the five patterns of major 7th, minor 7th, and dominant 7th chord shapes up and down the fingerboard.
- To play "basic moves."
- To play rhythmic progressions.

In Chapter 21 we learned the major 7th, minor 7th, and dominant 7th chord shapes in fingering patterns 1, 2, and 4. Let's now add the shapes of patterns 3 and 5 to complete the patterns for these chord types.

It is important to learn as many shapes as possible. So far you have covered many voicings for each chord type. This is good, but we must stay on top of them, so make sure you keep time in your practice schedule for regular review. See how many ways you can think of to play any chord type, then look in this book for the ones that escaped your mind. Put extra emphasis on chords you don't always remember. Challenge your mind as well as your fingers.

Major 7th Chord Shapes

Figure 50 shows the Cmaj7 chord shapes in patterns 3 and 5.

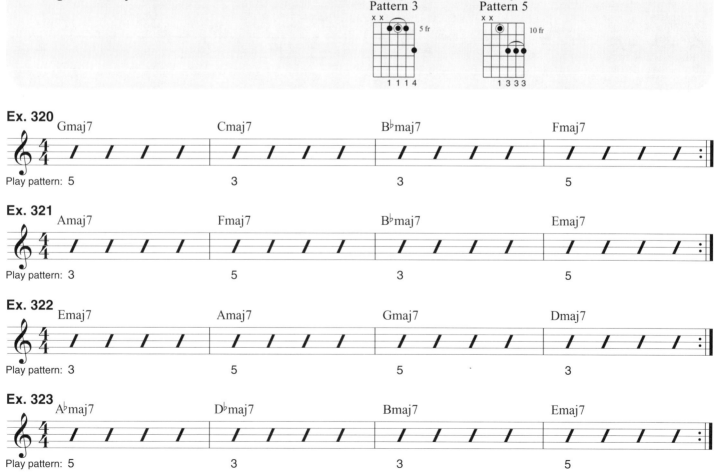

Fig. 50: Cmaj7 chords

Dominant 7th Chord Shapes

Figure 51 shows the C7 chord shapes in patterns 3 and 5.

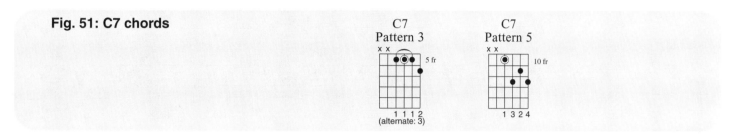

Fig. 51: C7 chords

Ex. 324

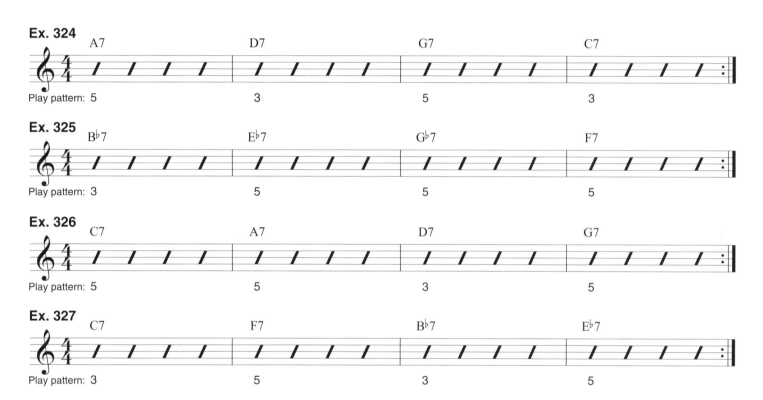

Minor 7th Chord Shapes

Figure 52 shows the Cm7 chord shapes in patterns 3 and 5.

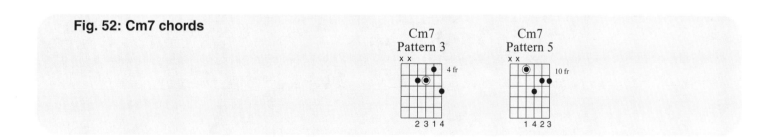

Fig. 52: Cm7 chords

"Basic Moves"

The following "basic moves" all use the major 7th, minor 7th, and dominant 7th chord shapes learned in this chapter. You decide which chord shapes to play, making sure to keep all roots within a six fret range of each other.

Ex. 332

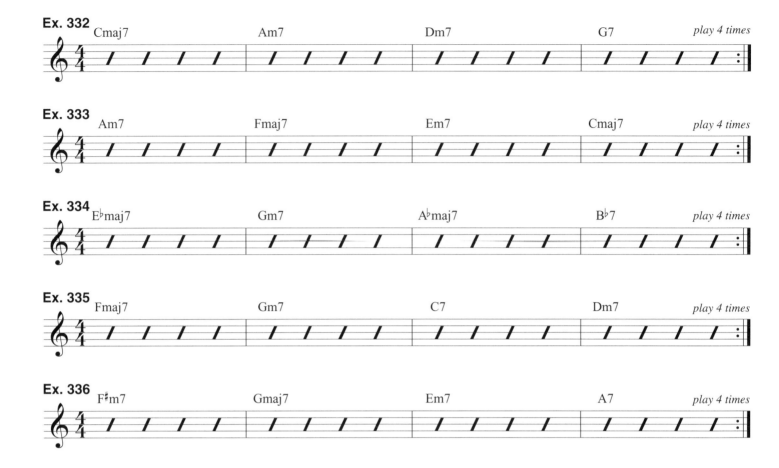

Connecting the Patterns

The following exercises simply connect the patterns of major 7th, minor 7th, and dominant 7th chord shapes. The three exercises below use C as the root, but you should ultimately be able to play these in all keys.

Play the chords in half notes at a moderate tempo ($\quarternote = 80$), until the chord connections are smooth up and down the fingerboard.

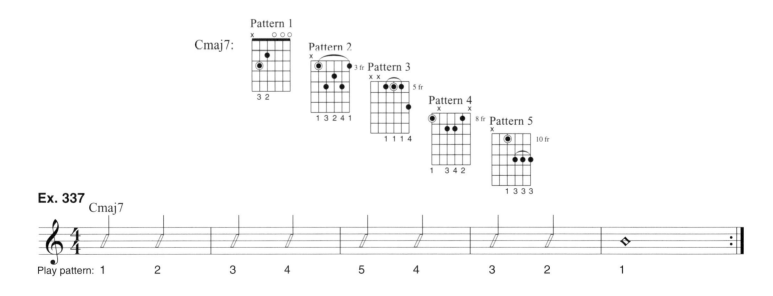

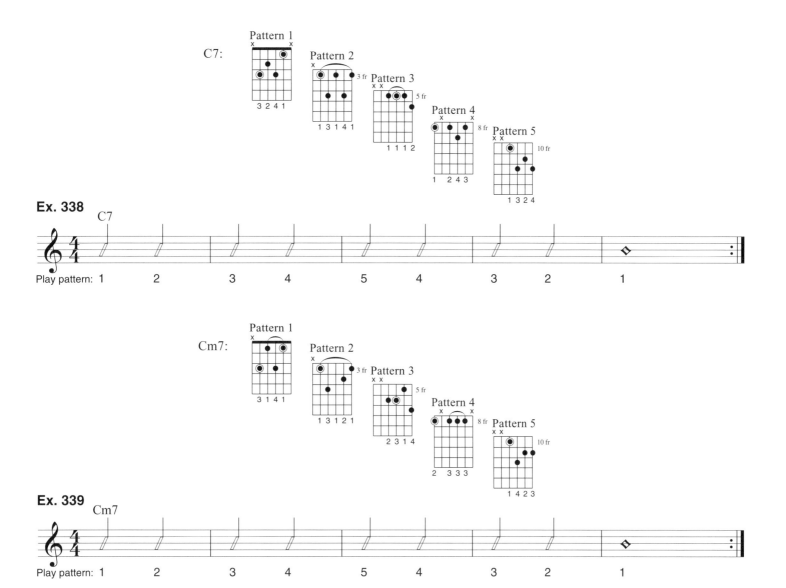

Ex. 338

Play pattern: 1   2   3   4   5   4   3   2   1

Ex. 339

Play pattern: 1   2   3   4   5   4   3   2   1

Progressions

The following progressions use the major 7th, minor 7th, and dominant 7th chord shapes presented in this chapter. As a general rule remember to keep all roots of chords within a six fret range. Use the suggested rhythm patterns given with each progression and pay close attention to repeats, multiple endings, and codas.

Begin with the voicings in this chapter, then incorporate all voicings learned. Try to eventually work out a set of voicings for each progression—one you have thought over and can repeat exactly the same way each time. Think of the highest note in each chord, how does it sound? Should that high note go up for the next voicing or down? What direction is the melody note going to take? You should control the sound of the chords to the way you want to hear them. Experiment!

Finally there is space at the end of the chapter to *write your own progression*. Do so! If you *write*, you will *learn*.

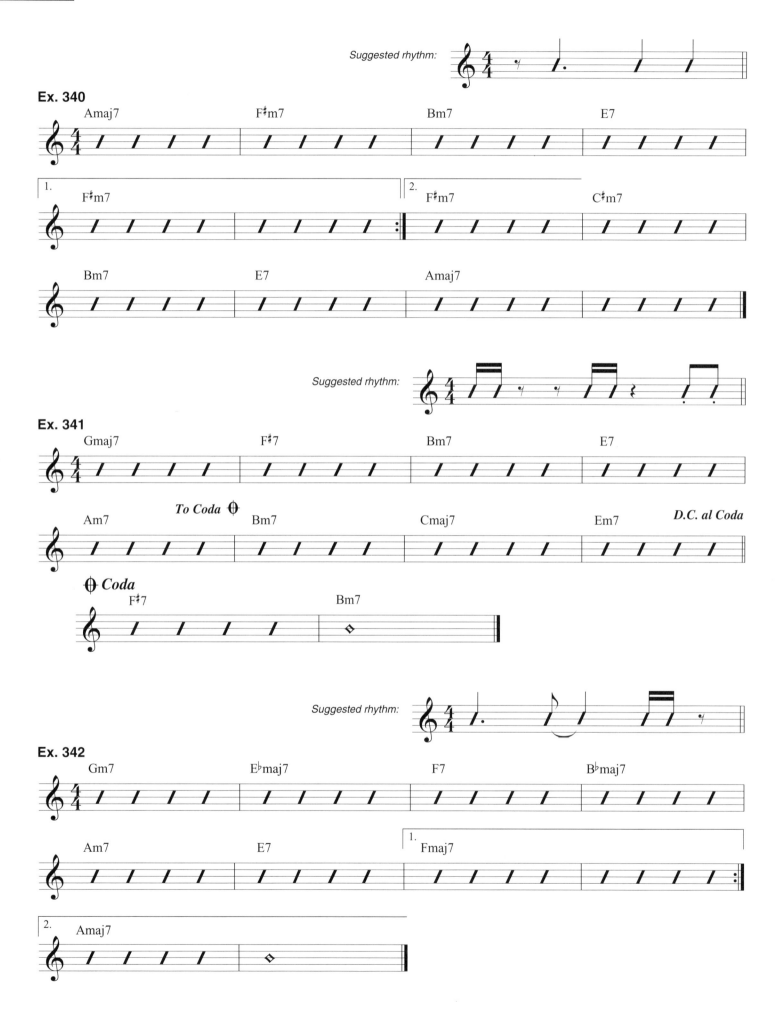

Now write your own progression (or progressions).

Chapter Twenty-Three

Inversions

Triads are three-note chords constructed from the first, third, and fifth notes of the major scale. A *voicing* is the order in which the notes are arranged upward from the bass note.

An *inversion* refers to which note is in the bass. However, with triads the most common inversions are achieved by simply raising the lowest note up one octave.

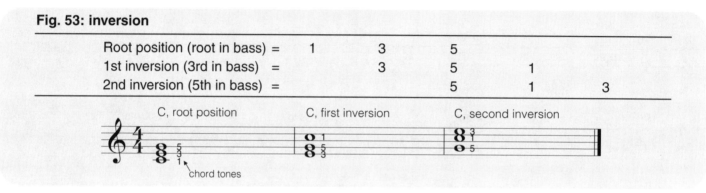

Fig. 53: inversion

Root position (root in bass) =	1	3	5
1st inversion (3rd in bass) =		3	5	1
2nd inversion (5th in bass) =			5	1	3

In this chapter, we will look at three-note chord shapes and their inversions on the top three strings (1, 2, 3) and the next lower set of strings (2, 3, 4).

These string sets are the most practical for playing in a band situation. Because they cut through the mix well and offer a different texture than barre chords or open position chords, they are used quite often by the professional guitarist. They also further help us connect the positions and fifth are located, and help in the connection process of chords, arpeggios, and scales.

Major Triads

Fig. 54: C major triads on the top three strings

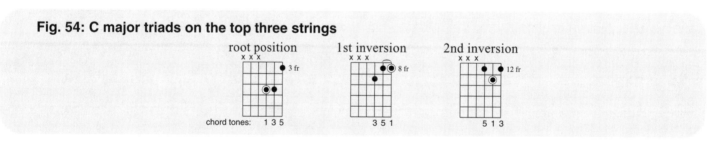

Keep all chords on the same set of strings (1, 2, 3). Below, inversions are writtten as "slash chords," with the chord name followed by the bass note. Inverted chords may not always be written as slash chords, but this does help identify the position on the neck. Practice this set of inversions for all roots, then use them in the following progressions.

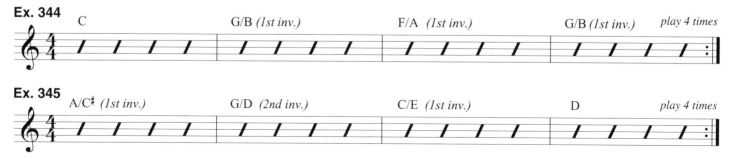

Fig. 55: C major triads on strings 2, 3, and 4

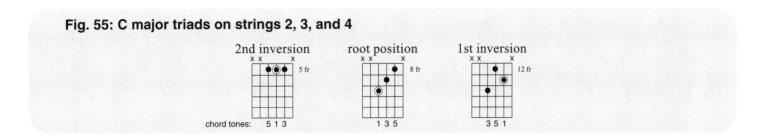

First, practice this set of inversions for all roots, then use them in the progressions below. Be sure to mute strings that are not supposed to sound!

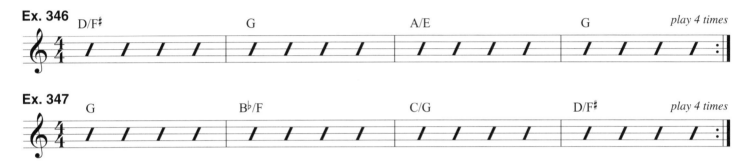

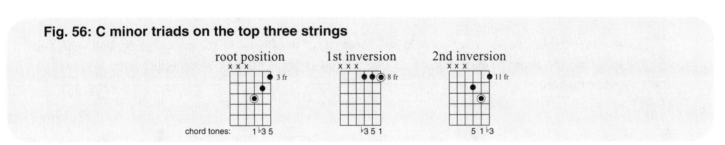

Minor Triads

Fig. 56: C minor triads on the top three strings

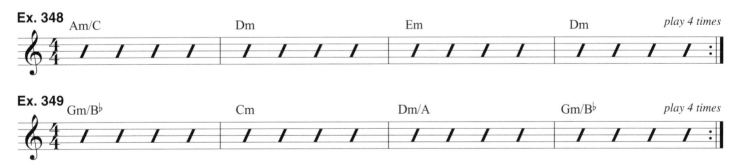

First, practice this set of inversions for all roots, then use them in the progressions below. NOTE: Major and minor are combined in example 349.

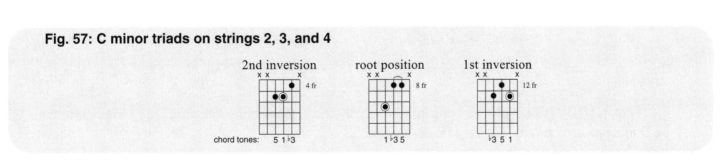

Fig. 57: C minor triads on strings 2, 3, and 4

First, practice this set of inversions for all roots, then use them in the the progressions below.

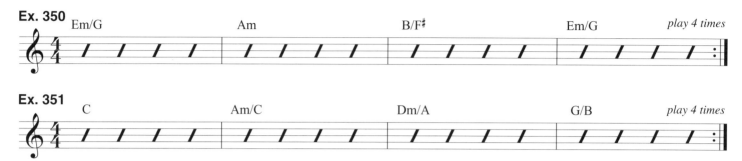

Augmented Triads

Below are the shapes for augmented triads on the top three strings. Compare these to the major shapes and notice the raised fifth.

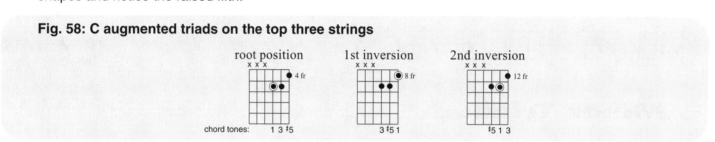

Fig. 58: C augmented triads on the top three strings

First, practice this set of inversions for all roots, then use them in the progression below. A "+" symbol following the chord name indicates an augmented chord. Use the diagrams provided to draw out the shapes, if needed.

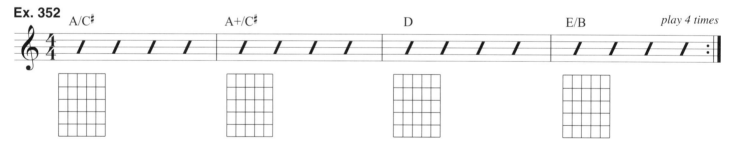

Here are the shapes for C augmented on strings 2, 3, and 4. Compare these to the C major shapes and see the raised fifth.

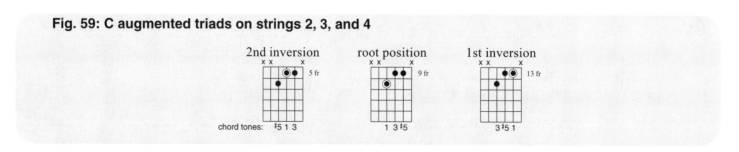

Fig. 59: C augmented triads on strings 2, 3, and 4

First, practice this set of inversions for all roots, then use them in the following progression. Use the diagrams provided to draw out the shapes, if needed.

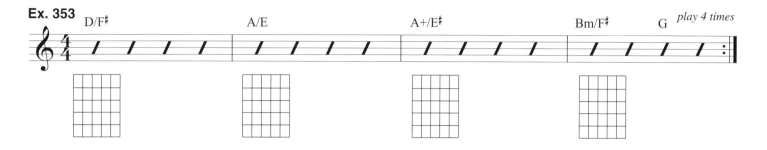

Ex. 353 D/F♯   A/E   A+/E♯   Bm/F♯   G *play 4 times*

Diminished Triads

Below are the shapes for C diminished on the top three strings. Compare these to minor and see the lowered fifth.

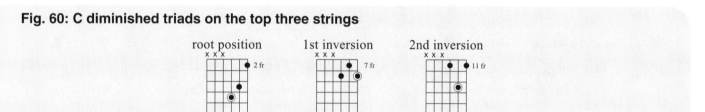

Fig. 60: C diminished triads on the top three strings

root position   1st inversion   2nd inversion

chord tones: 1 ♭3 ♭5   ♭3 ♭5 1   ♭5 1 ♭3

First, practice this set of inversions for all roots, then use them in the progression below. A "°" symbol indicates a diminished chord.

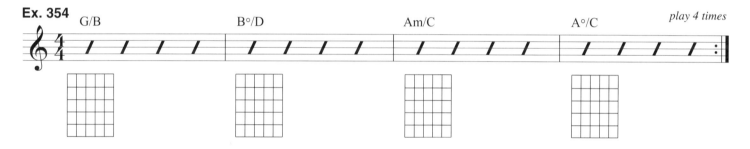

Ex. 354 G/B   B°/D   Am/C   A°/C   *play 4 times*

Here are the shapes for C diminished on strings 2, 3, and 4. Compare these to C minor and see the lowered fifth.

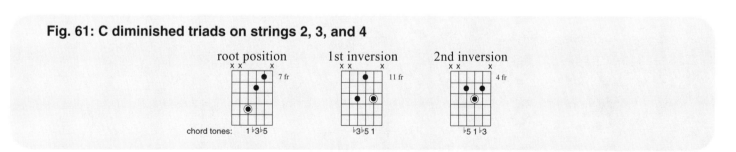

Fig. 61: C diminished triads on strings 2, 3, and 4

root position   1st inversion   2nd inversion

chord tones: 1 ♭3 ♭5   ♭3 ♭5 1   ♭5 1 ♭3

First, practice this set of inversions for all roots, then use them in the progression below.

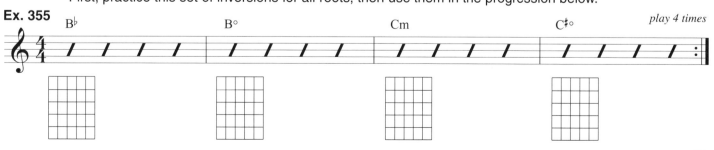

Ex. 355 B♭   B°   Cm   C♯°   *play 4 times*

Points to Remember

- Learning these shapes may take some time, but the rewards are well worth the effect. These shapes will unlock a lot of the mystery of the guitar neck. They should be practiced daily and reviewed often. Use the progressions provided in this chapter, but write some of your own, too.

- Think of different ways to practice these shapes and incorporate them into your arpeggio and scale studies. Memorize the location of each chord tone in every diagram so you know where the root, third, and fifth of every chord is located.

- The smaller triad shapes should also be seen as part of the larger shapes already learned.

- Play all shapes as both single-note arpeggios and arpeggiated chords (by holding the shape and letting the notes ring together).

- Make sure you learn major and minor first, then see augmented as a variation of major and diminished as a variation of minor.

- Play the chords cleanly and make sure to mute the strings not played. Be able to play loudly and softly. Dynamics will help make chords sound more effective.

- Combine the top set of three strings with the second set (strings 2, 3, 4) after each set is mastered. Do this by using common progressions already practiced in this book. Then write some of your own!

Notes:

Chapter Twenty-Four

24

More Triad Inversions

In this chapter, we will finish the triad inversions on the lower two string groups. The *third set* of strings consists of strings 3, 4, and 5. The *fourth* set consists of strings 4, 5, and 6.

The chords on these lower two sets are not as practical for playing in a band situation. However, they are very necessary in order to complete your view of the neck and for seeing the relationships between roots, arpeggios, chords, and scales. Also there are a couple of voicings on the third set that *do* work in a band situation when used in combination with the second set.

It should also be stated that the purpose of knowing these shapes is to memorize the location of all possible roots, thirds, and fifths on the neck, regardless of what position you're in. It may seem tedious at first, but the reward is that you will truly understand the neck and later, as you study more advanced chords, you will more easily see where they come from. Remember: root, third, and fifth make up the skeleton everything else "hangs" from!

NOTE: The augmented and diminished triads will not be shown for these lower string sets but you can figure them out because you know the theory behind them. See augmented in relation to major (raise the fifth), and see diminished in relation to minor (lower the fifth).

Here are the shapes for C major and C minor on the lowest set (4th) set of strings. *Observe the thirds.* This is the only difference between major and minor.

Fig. 62: C major triads on lowest three strings

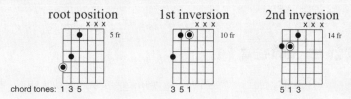

Fig. 63: C minor triads on the lowest three strings

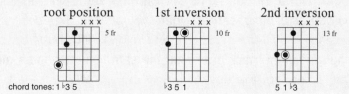

Practice tips:

- Pick three roots a day, change to three different roots the next day.
- Practice in all keys—first major then minor.
- Compare major and minor chords of the same inversion, then move it up to the next inversion. Do this using several different roots.

Here are the shapes for C major and C minor on the third set of strings (3, 4, and 5). *Observe the thirds.*

Fig. 64: C major triads on strings 3, 4, and 5

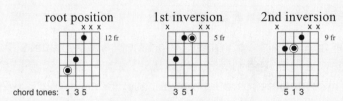

Fig. 65: C minor triads on strings 3, 4, and 5

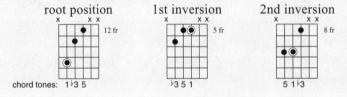

Practice tips:

- Practice in all keys—first major, then minor.

- Compare major and minor of the same inversion, then move up to the next inversion. Do this using several different roots.

- Combine the third and fourth sets.

"Across" the Neck

Now let's combine all four sets. By doing this you have played every possible root, third, and fifth on the neck for the chord in question. This is a different "direction" than moving up and down the four string-sets. This time, we are going *across* the four string-sets, and playing one inversion off each string-set. This create three groups.

The *first group* starts with the root on the sixth string. Then as you go across the neck in string-sets, playing each inversion, you arrive at the top string-set with the same voicing you started with (in this case 1–3–5). However, it is *one octave higher* than where you started. The *second group* starts with the third in the bass, then moves across. The *third group* starts with the fifth in the bass and moves across.

This method of moving across the neck gives you the same inversions as moving up the neck but in a different direction. This points out the essential way the guitar works—up and down the strings changing positions, and/or across the neck staying in one position. You have probably seen this with scales already, but chords and arpeggios do the same thing. This, once again helps form a connection between chord, arpeggio, and scale shapes.

There are two things at work here with triads and their inversions—memorizing the *shape* and memorizing the *location* of roots, thirds, and fifths. Look at both! This is something that must be practiced on a regular basis. Just look at three roots a day, but do it daily. If you hang in there and work these shapes out, you will have great insight to how the guitar is set up and eventually be able to use these shapes without much thought. But it takes a little hard work at first is to practice them daily and see them regardless of where you start on the neck. Also play progressions, using rhythm and style, to make it musical after you have seen and practiced the mechanical relationships.

Points to Remember

- The top two sets work best in a band situation.
- The octave shapes discussed earlier show all the roots. Now you are taking on the thirds and fifths.
- Moving up and down each set of strings is direction #1.
- Moving across the strings is direction #2.
- Apply the chords to progressions and write your own as well.
- Practice daily.

Fig. 66: C major, "across the neck"

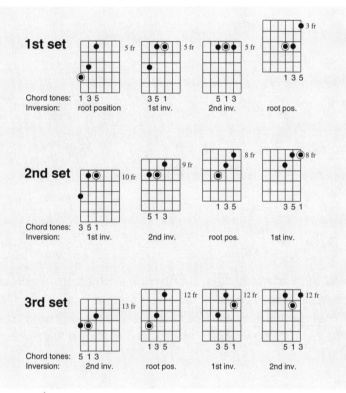

Fig. 67: C minor, "across the neck"

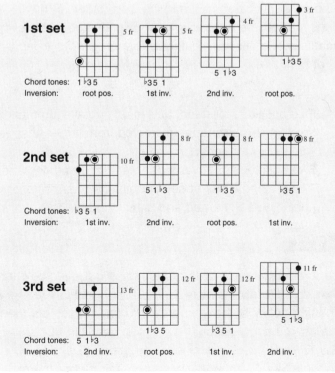

Chapter Twenty-Five

Rhythm and Interpretation

Much of what is called the "feel" of a song or style is contained in the rhythm, as well as the types of chords and the way you attack the strings. Rhythm starts with the basic pulse, but you have different ways to interpret the pulse in terms of its subdivision (that is, different ways of breaking up the beat).

Common Subdivisions:

1. Quarter note (walking)
2. Eighth note (straight)
3. Eighth note (shuffle/swing)
4. Eighth note triplet (3/8, 6/8, 9/8)
5. Sixteenth note (straight)
6. Sixteenth note (swing)

Below is a list of common styles. Fill in the basic feel (subdivision) they most often use.

Rock _____ Country _____ Funk _____ Blues _____

Jazz _____ Folk/Acoustic _____ Pop _____

Hip hop _____ Metal _____ Fusion _____

It is through the combined effect of this subdivision—which to us should mean some type of groove/strum—and the particular chord voicings, that we create a "sound" or "feel." Try playing the same progression or song but change the tempo, subdivision, and type of chords. Listen to how different it sounds. You must inject the music with whatever "feel" there is. Learn the different ideas presented here and apply them in your practicing.

Review

We have studied a lot of chord shapes in the last few chapters and now it's time for review and application. The student should always be involved with application of newly learned material. In this chapter there are suggestions that can be applied to your own situation. However, in the long run it is the dedicated and vigilant student who is always looking and seeing ways to apply all the learned shapes and theoretical possibilities at hand.

So far…

Chapter 19:	Five positions for major and minor, octave jump exercise.
Chapter 20:	Voicings (small shapes extracted from larger shapes), in five positions with their variations.
Chapters 21 and 22:	Five positions of 7th chords (maj7, m7, and dominant 7th).
Chapters 23 and 24:	Three-string triads (4 sets), locations of all roots, thirds, and fifths (including augmented and diminished triads).

Practice Tips

Organize your practice to address each of these topics; if not everyday, then at least half one day and the other half the next day. Rotate days with these subjects. Nothing works quite as well as repetition! If you are truly getting better at these chords and chord systems then it should take you less time to cover these subjects as you continue. Just don't stop practicing because you *think* you know the information. Find some way to find a new exercise or progression and keep coming back to the new chords until they feel comfortable to you. Then you can begin to practice them!

Rhythmic Interpretation

In these following progressions, think of the rhythmic possibilities (subdivision, anticipation, tempo, groove/strum), as well as the harmonic possibilities (voicings, texture/tone, density, strings, register).

When looking at basic charts that have *hash marks* you are free to interpret in a way that is stylisticly correct and rhythmically correct! What makes that happen? Talk about the feel for each of the following progressions. What about the rhythm? What about the voicings? The subdivision? The tempo? Dynamics? Accents? Style?

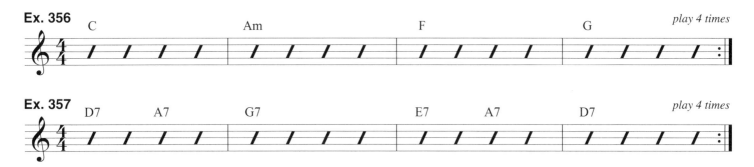

Play steady, even eighth notes on distorted power chords. Use all downstrokes, slightly muted.

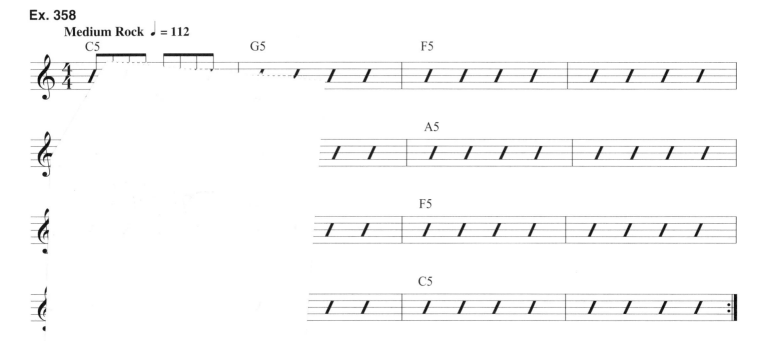

ommon groove with steady eighth notes. Now, let's create an
draw out some accents. Use chord voicings other than the power
I the strumming on the accompanying part be legato, staccato, or
eating a part, explore different possibilities before settling on one

ape deck or with another student and perform/record it. Then, write
he following page.

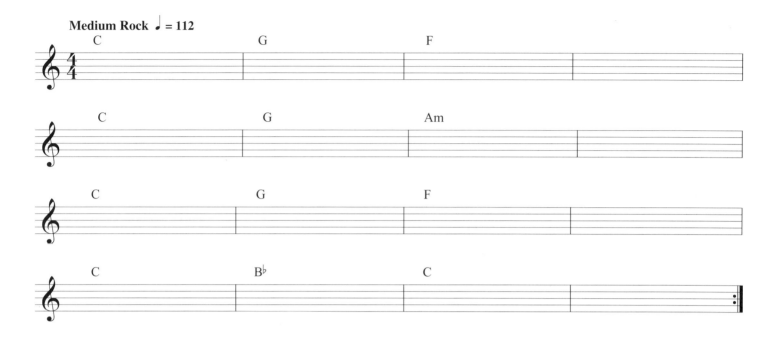

Now let's try some other rhythmic approaches. Play the following progression with the ties as indicated.

Ex. 359

Now, change the placement of the ties and notice the subtle shift in the feel.

Ex. 360

Example 361 is a fast, upbeat, straight-eighth note "Ska" feel.

Ex. 361

Here is a slower, swing-eighth reggae.

Ex. 362

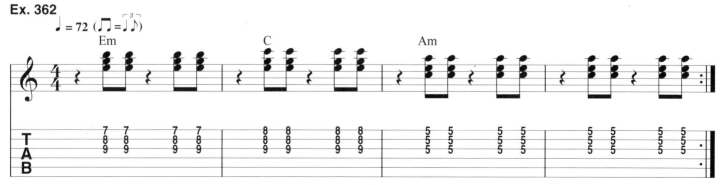

In example 363, experiment with tempo and straight or swing-eighths.

Ex. 363

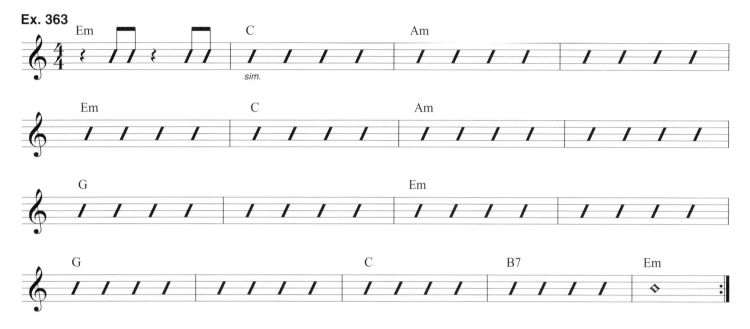

Play the first attack of each bar short (staccato) and the second attack accent louder.

Ex. 364

Play the following progression along with a drummer or drum machine playing a *half time rock feel*. That would put the backbeat once per measure, on beat 3.

Ex. 365
Moderate Rock
Half-Time Feel

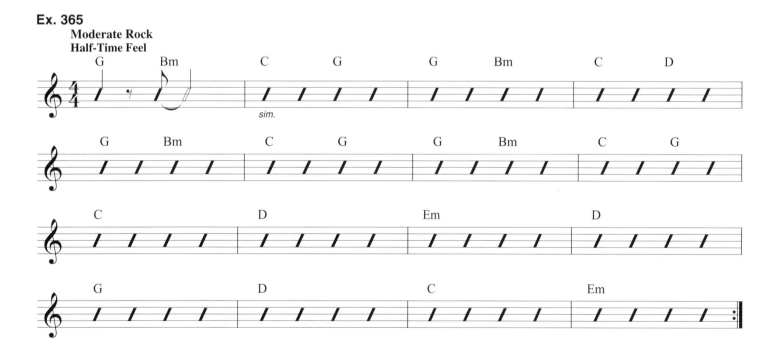

Now play that same rhythmic figure, but this time over walking 4/4 jazz swing feel (both slow and fast tempos). Observe how the feel changed even though you used the same figure.

Ex. 366

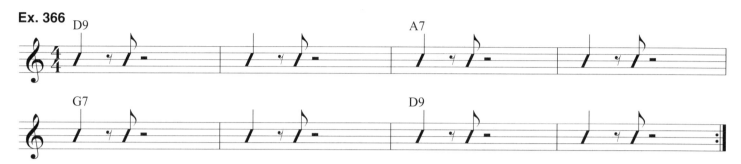

Next, slow it down and play the basic rhythmic figure with a slow ballad feel. Keep it steady and relaxed, in the slower eighth-note groove.

Ex. 367

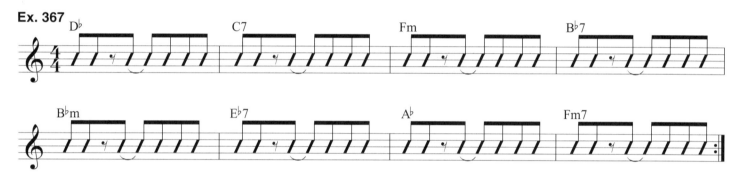

Progressions

Apply all the ideas presented to the following progressions.

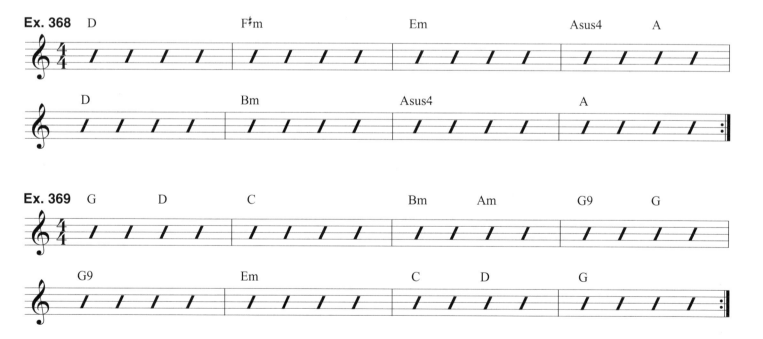

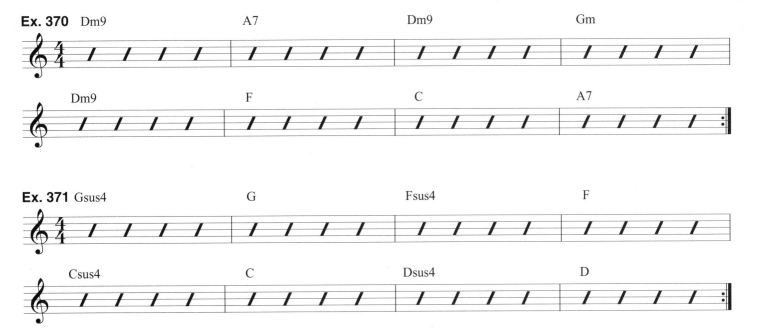

Ex. 370

| Dm9 | A7 | Dm9 | Gm |

| Dm9 | F | C | A7 |

Ex. 371

| Gsus4 | G | Fsus4 | F |

| Csus4 | C | Dsus4 | D |

Notes:

Chapter Twenty-Six

Objectives

- To learn the location of chord tones within the scale tones for pattern 4.
- To learn to play the harmonized scale.
- To play diatonic progressions utilizing Roman Numeral symbols.

In this chapter, we will learn the location of scale tones in fingering pattern 4 and extract the chord tones from the scale pattern. With these chord tones, we will then build major 7th, minor 7th, dominant 7th, and minor 7♭5 chord "voicings" within this pattern.

If you know the formula for constructing a chord, you can then arrange those chord tones in almost any order and obtain a particular voicing. The trick is to know what the common voicings are and be able to hear the difference between two chords that are of the same chord type but still sound slightly different because the voicings are different.

Certain voicings will work better in certain situations. Also, changing the voicing of just one particular chord during a progression gives more variety to the overall sound of the progression.

Here is fingering pattern 4. Learn the numbers and then build some voicings!

Fingering Pattern 4

Fig. 68: scale shape and tones in pattern 4, with roots on sixth, fourth, and first strings

shape    scale tones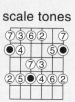

Now, draw the chord shapes for these voicings.

major 7th 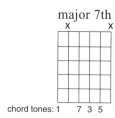   dominant 7th 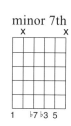   minor 7th 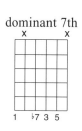   minor 7♭5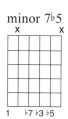

chord tones: 1 7 3 5   1 ♭7 3 5   1 ♭7 ♭3 5   1 ♭7 ♭3 ♭5

The Harmonized Scale

The process of building triads and/or 7th chords on the degrees of the major scale, using only the pitches found within that scale, is called *harmonizing* the scale. By taking the 1, 7, 3, 5 chord voicing from pattern 4, we can apply it to each scale degree using the necessary chord type found within the harmonized scale. Therefore we will have used the same voicing for each chord.

Fig. 69: seventh chords of the harmonized major scale

CHORD TYPE:	maj7	m7	m7	maj7	dom.7	m7	m7♭5
Scale degrees:	I	ii	iii	IV	V	vi	viiø

Play the F harmonized major scale.

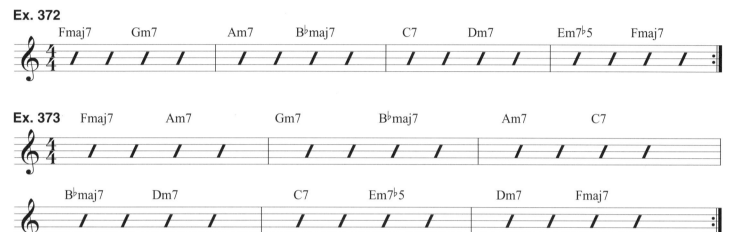

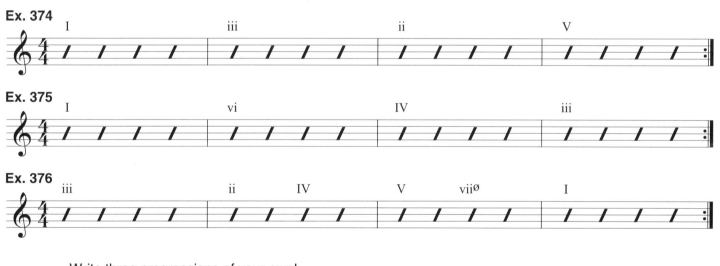

The next few exercises use Roman Numerals only to indicate the chords. They may be played in any key using the same voicings you drew at the start of this chapter. In some keys, voicings that were higher on the neck will eventually get too high for practical use, but they will reappear in the lower register.

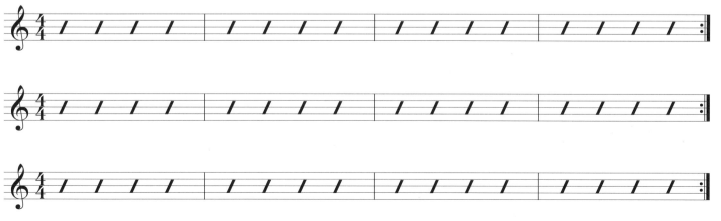

Write three progressions of your own!

Exercises

In the blank diagrams below, draw each of the following voicings in pattern 4 with the root on the sixth string. With the extra diagrams, create some of your own voicings.

1. Major 6th   1–6–3–5
2. Dom. 7th   1–5–♭7–3–♭7
3. Minor 7th   1–5–♭7–♭3–5
4. Minor 9th   1–5–♭7–♭3–♭7–9
5. Major 6/9   1–3–6–9–5
6. Major 9th   3–1–9–5–7 (1st inversion)*

•root is on fourth string and third is on fifth string in Pattern #4

In the blank diagrams below, draw the following voicings in pattern 4 with the root on the fourth string. Again, create some of your own voicings, too.

1. Major 7th   1–3–5–7
2. Dom. 7th   1–3–♭7–1
3. Minor 9th   1–♭3–♭7–9

Notes:

Chapter Twenty-Seven

Objectives

- To learn the location of chord tones within the scale tones for pattern 2.
- To learn the harmonized scale using pattern 2 shapes.
- To play diatonic progressions utilizing Roman Numeral symbols.

In this chapter, we will learn the location of scale tones from fingering pattern 2 and then extract the chord tones from the scale pattern. With these chord tones, we will then build major 7th, minor 7th, dominant 7th, and minor 7♭5 chord "voicings" within this pattern.

Again, if you know the formula for constructing a chord you can then arrange those chord tones in almost any order and obtain a particular voicing. Certain voicings will work better in certain situations. Also changing the voicing of a particular chord during the progression gives more variety to the overall sound of the progression.

Fingering Pattern 2

Here is fingering pattern 2. Learn the numbers and then build some voicings!

Fig. 70: scale shape and tones in pattern 2, with roots on fifth and third strings

scale shape

scale tones

Draw the chord shapes for these voicings in pattern 2.

major 7th

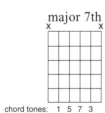

dominant 7th

minor 7th

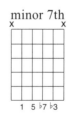

minor 7♭5

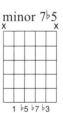

chord tones: 1 5 7 3   1 5 ♭7 3   1 5 ♭7 ♭3   1 ♭5 ♭7 ♭3

The Harmonized Scale, with Pattern 2 Shapes

Next, we will harmonize the major scale using pattern 2 chord shapes.

Fig. 71: chords of the harmonized major scale

CHORD TYPE:	maj7	m7	m7	maj7	dom.7	m7	m7♭5
Scale degrees:	I	ii	iii	IV	V	vi	viiØ

Play the B♭ harmonized scale, below, using the pattern 2 chord shapes.

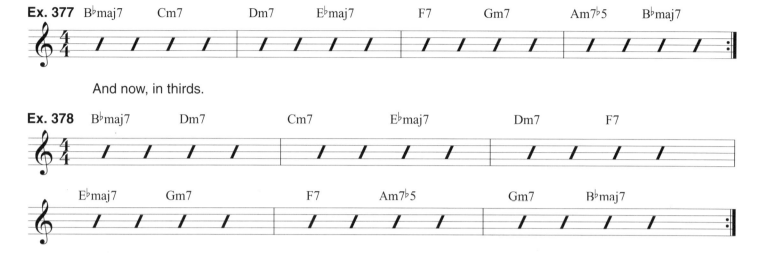

And now, in thirds.

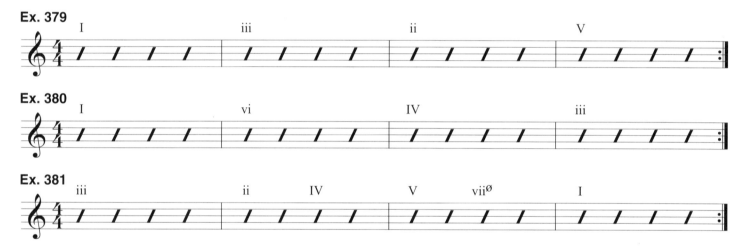

The next few exercises use Roman Numerals only. They may be played in any key using the same voicings you drew at the start of this chapter. In some keys, voicings that were higher on the neck will eventually get too high for practical use, but will reappear in the lower register.

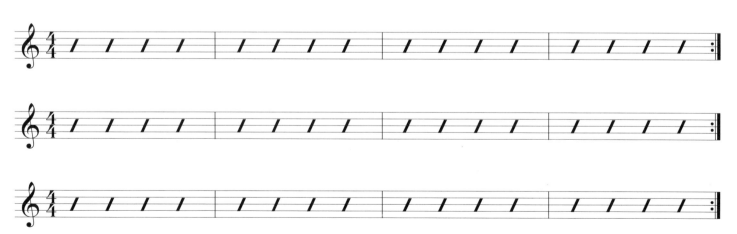

Write three progressions of your own!

Exercise

Draw out the following voicings in pattern 2, using the diagrams below. With the extra diagrams, create some of your own voicings.

1.	Major 7th	1–7–3–5
2.	Major 7th	1–5–1–3–7
3.	Major 6/9	1–3–6–9–5
4.	Major 6th	1–5–6–3
5.	Minor 6th	1–6–♭3–5
6.	Minor 7th	1–♭7–♭3–5
7.	Minor 9th	1–♭3–♭7–9(5) (optional fifth on top)
8.	Dom. 7th	1–♭7–3–5
9.	Minor 7♭5	1–♭7–♭3–♭5

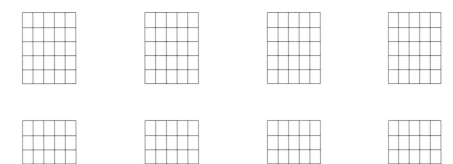

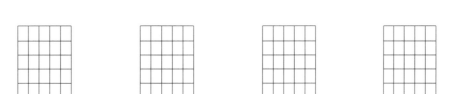

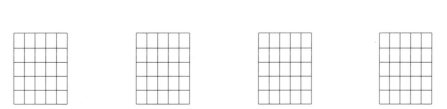

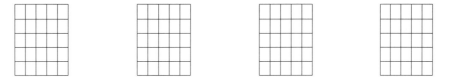

Notes:

Chapter Twenty-Eight

Objectives

- To learn the location of chord tones within the scale tones for pattern 5.
- To learn the harmonized scale, using pattern 5 chord shapes.
- To play diatonic progressions utilizing Roman Numeral symbols.

In this chapter, we will learn the location of scale tones from fingering pattern 5 and then extract the chord tones from that scale pattern. With these chord tones, we will then build major 7th, minor 7th, dominant 7th, and minor 7♭5 chord voicings within this pattern.

Fingering Pattern 5

Here is fingering pattern 5. Learn the numbers and then build some voicings!

Fig. 72: scale shape and tones in pattern 5, with roots on the sixth, fourth, and second strings

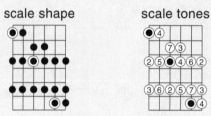

Draw the chord tones for these voicings.

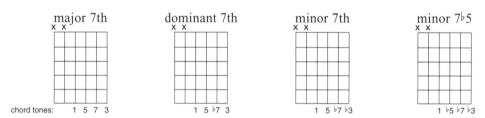

The Harmonized Scale, with Pattern 5 Shapes

Now, let's harmonize the major scale using pattern 5 chord shapes. Again, the sequence of chord types relative to the Roman Numerals is the same:

Fig. 73: chords of the harmonized major scale

CHORD TYPE:	maj7	m7	m7	maj7	dom.7	m7	m7♭5
Scale degrees:	I	ii	iii	IV	V	vi	viiø

Play the E♭ harmonized scale, using pattern 5 chord shapes.

Ex. 382

And in thirds…

Ex. 383

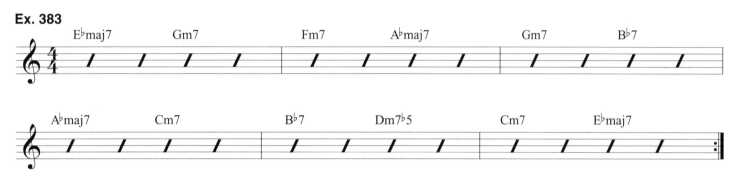

NOTE: Voicing 1–5–7–3 from pattern 5, root on the fourth string, is the same as 1–5–7–3 from pattern 2, root on the fifth string.

The next few exercises use Roman Numerals only. They may be played in any key using the same voicings you drew at the start of this chapter. In some keys, voicings that were higher on the neck will eventually get too high for practical use, but will reappear in the lower register.

Ex. 384

Ex. 385

Ex. 386

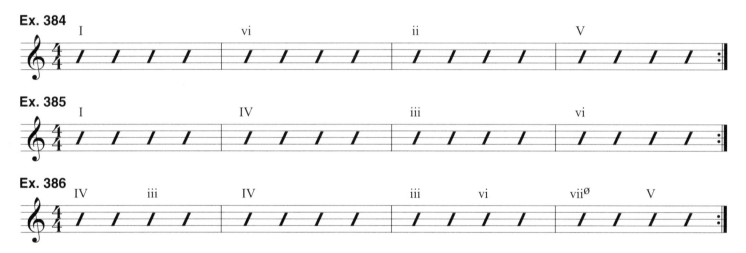

Write three progressions of your own!

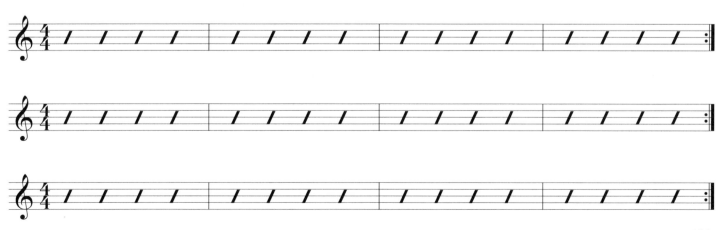

Exercise

Finally, draw out the following voicings in pattern 5. With the extra diagrams, create some of your own voicings.

1.	Major 6th	1–5–6–3
2.	Minor 6th	1–5–6–♭3
3.	Dom. 9th	1–3–♭7–9
4.	Dom. 7sus4	1–5–♭7–4
5.	Minor	1–5–1–♭3
6.	Major 7th	3–1–5–7*
7.	Dom. 7th	3–1–5–♭7*
8.	Major 9th	1–3–7–9
9.	Major	3–1–5–1*
10.	Major 7th	1–5–3–7 (3) (optional third on top)

•third is on sixth string and root on fourth string for these inversions

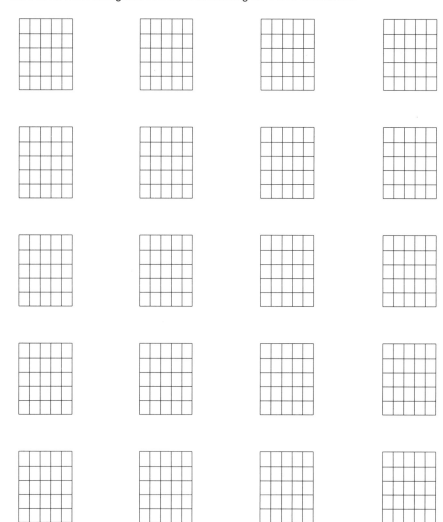

Notes:

Chapter Twenty-Nine

Combined String-Sets for Harmonized Scales

So far we have looked at three ways to play the chords in the harmonized scale:

- Voicing 1–7–3–5, root on sixth string.
- Voicing 1–5–7–3, root on fifth string.
- Voicing 1–5–7–3, root on fourth string.

This approach emphasizes moving up the neck, along one string, from each scale degree to the next. This is a valid way to see the neck play chords. However it is only half of the picture. The other half is the concept of staying in a position and playing "across" the neck.

In this chapter, we will concentrate on the "position" concept and combine the already learned harmonized scales to create an "in position" set of chords for a key. If we think of the "I" chord and its starting position, we will then have two sets of chords: one starting with the root on the sixth string, and the other starting with the root on the fifth string.

There are a variety a voicings possible in any given position. On the next few pages, we will use the 1–7–3–5 and 1–5–7–3 voicings. These should be thought of as a solid place to start, a kind of "skeleton" of the key. The next step would be to find other voicings related to this "skeleton." You have looked at many voicings in the last couple of chapters, including extended chords. You should begin to add these other voicings to your "skeleton" and create different colors by using different voicings. However, you can always rely on the basic chords presented here to know a key and be able to think of the progression in Roman Numerals. You must experiment and use your ear!

It should also be stated that using only triads (whether large five and six string voicings or smaller three string voicings) to play the harmonized scale is also very common. You should be able to play through any key using triads only. Finally you should then combine triads, 7ths, and/or 6th chords. You will only be able to recognize the sounds if you work hard at creating the sounds. Each voicing has its own character and eventually can be recognized by ear.

Fig. 74: harmonized A major scale, with sixth string "I" chord

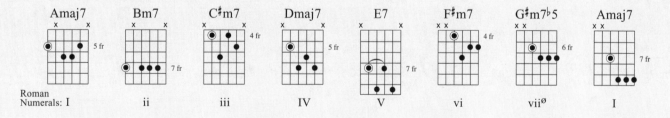

Fig. 75: harmonized D major scale, with fifth string "I" chord

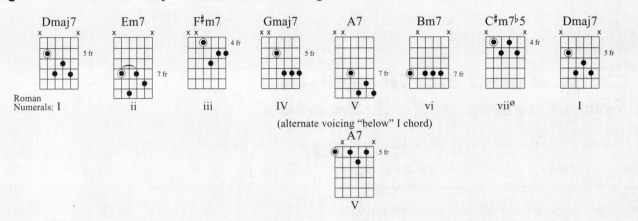

Now practice these "in position" harmonized scale patterns in all keys. Once the shapes have been learned, play and say the name of each chord in the key. Be sure to do this in all keys in order to familiarize yourself with all the keys. Do this exercise with both sets of chords, (the one that starts with the "I" on the sixth string root, then the "I" chord starting on the 5th string root).

Then work out the harmonized scales using triad shapes for both the sixth and fifth string "I" chord starting points.

Progressions

Practice these progressions first in the indicated key, then in all keys using the Roman Numerals as your guide.

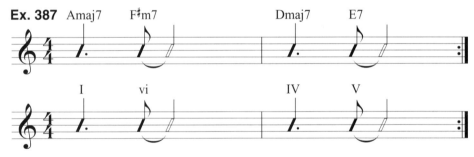

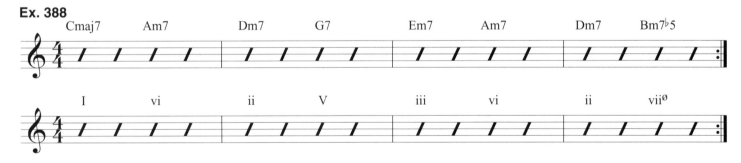

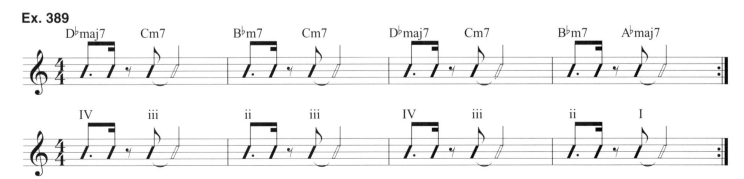

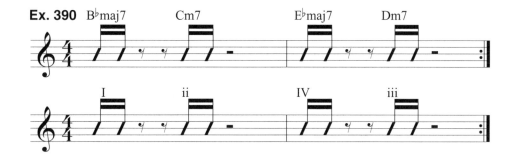

Exercise 391 uses triads only.

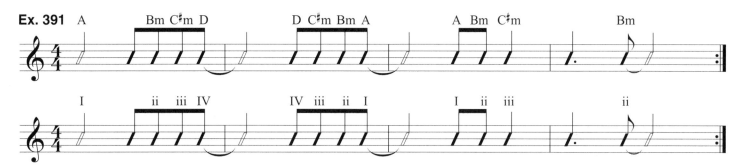

Write out a few diatonic progressions of your own, below. Use different chord types (triad, 6th, 7th, 9th, etc.) but keep it diatonic. You may also write rhythm figures that go along with the chords. This definitely helps the progression come alive!

Chapter Thirty
30

Sixteenth Note Strumming

In this chapter, we are going to concentrate on the picking hand. The main objective here is to achieve a relaxed, even stroke. Practicing with a metronome is essential. Usually each style can be related to a certain groove; in this chapter we will use common sixteenth note scratch figures. All exercises should be practiced first with straight sixteenths as the subdivision, and then again with "swing" sixteenths. Strive to find the "pocket" (that *relaxed* place!) in the rhythm.

Play these exercises while muting with the fretting hand. Focus on being relaxed and even.

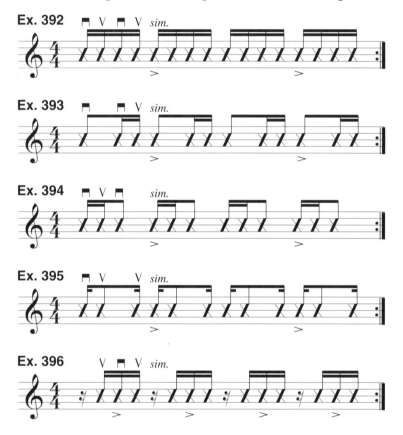

One-Bar Patterns

These one-bar patterns are to be practiced on a daily basis. The tempo should be changed from day to day. Use a metronome or drum machine to play along with. Concentrate on your time and voicings so you begin to play more relaxed in the hands and the mind.

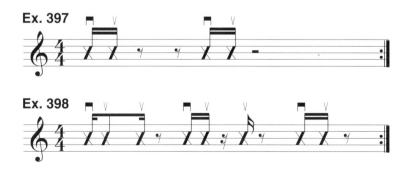

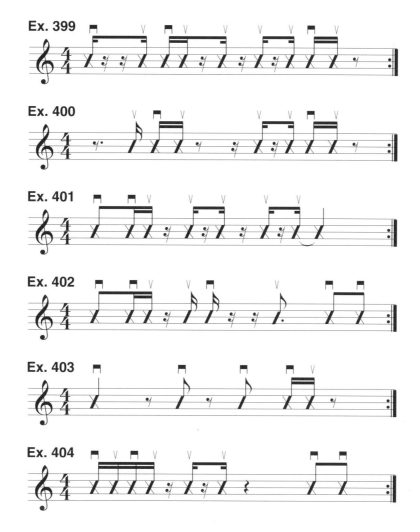

"Basic Moves"

These "basic moves" solve the problem of voicing so you can concentrate on mixing and matching the one-bar rhythm patterns with each "basic moves" example. Play as many as you can within the time you have allotted to practice, but don't rush through them. You can play a different set of one-bar patterns and "basic moves" each day. Vary your tempo between examples!

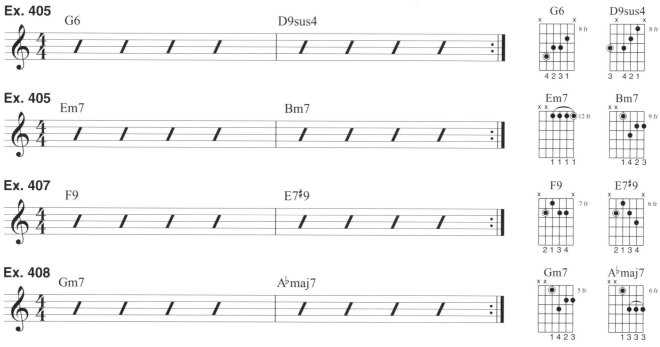

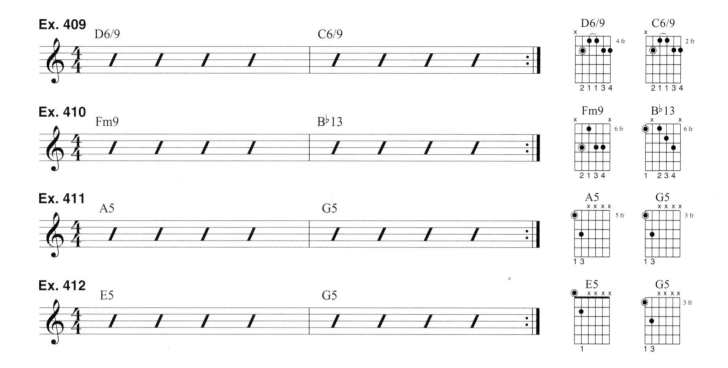

Ex. 409 D6/9 C6/9

Ex. 410 Fm9 B♭13

Ex. 411 A5 G5

Ex. 412 E5 G5

Progressions

The following progressions are meant to be payed in a variety of ways:

- Using full five or six string voicings (root position)
- Using three or four string voicings (inversions)

Ex. 413

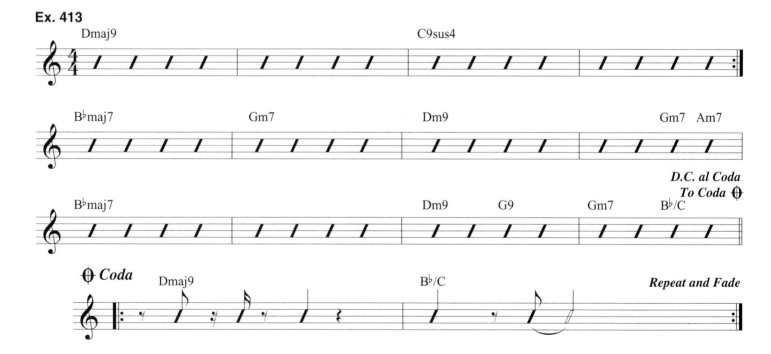

Dmaj9   C9sus4

B♭maj7   Gm7   Dm9   Gm7 Am7

D.C. al Coda
To Coda ⊕

B♭maj7   Dm9   G9   Gm7   B♭/C

⊕ *Coda*   Dmaj9   B♭/C   *Repeat and Fade*

Ex. 414

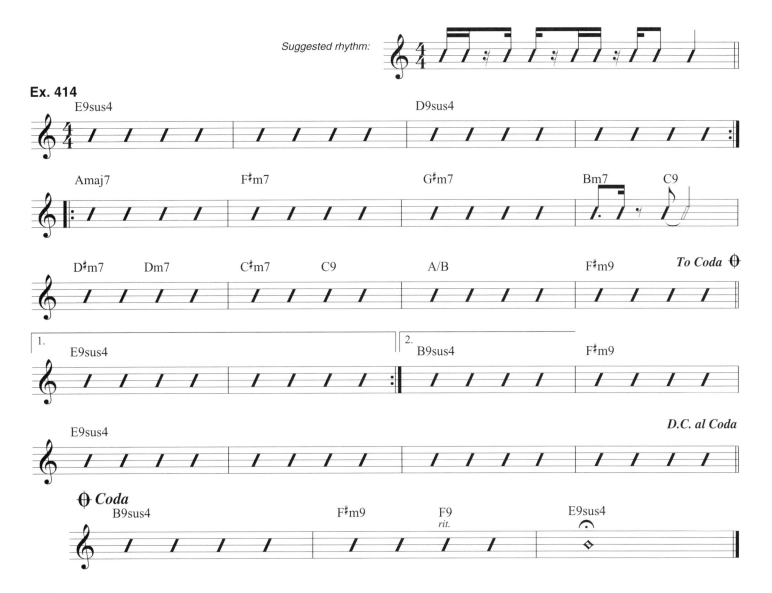

Notes:

Chapter Thirty-One

Writing Rhythms

The best way to develop your sense of rhythmic variety and phrasing is to create your own rhythmic patterns. In the last chapter, there were several one-bar rhythms you learned and practiced as accompaniment patterns. Use them as a reference for creating your own patterns. Don't forget to use rests and rhythmic anticipation, too. Also remember every recording you have is a gold mine of rhythms! Listen and you will notice rhythm is all around you.

Rhythm Exercise 1

Write an eighth note rhythm pattern that is one bar in length, for each of the following progressions.

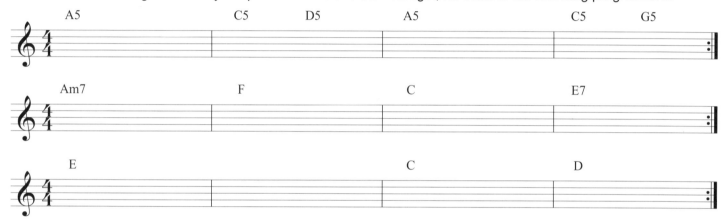

Rhythm Exercise 2

Write an eighth note rhythm pattern two bars in length, for each of the following progression.

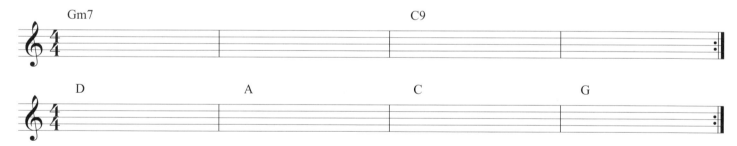

Rhythm Exercise 3

Write a sixteenth note rhythm pattern that is one bar in length, for the following progression.

Rhythm Exercise 4

Write a combination of eighth and sixteenth notes in a one- or two-bar rhythmic pattern.

Rhythm Exercise 5

Finally, write a little arrangement for the rhythm section in this song/progression. Indicate the rhythmic feel and write some ensemble "kicks" (rhythms to be accented by all rhythm section players).

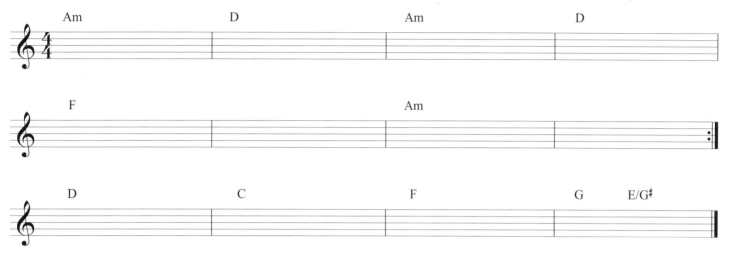

Altered chords

Altered chords are used to intensify the resolution from a "V" chord back to its intended "I" chord (whether major or minor). The two most common altered chords are probably the 7♭9 chord and the 7♯5 chords (+7 may also be used to represent the raised 5th in a dominant chord). These chords can seem rather tense and unstable by themselves, but, in combination with the chord that they resolve to (the I chord), they work. Always think of the altered chord in relation to the resolution chord.

Here are some voicings that are common for these two chord types.

Fig. 76: dominant and altered dominant chords

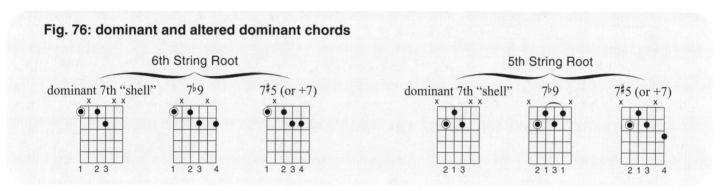

Now write a rhythm for exercise 6, below, and practice it using the altered dominant shapes you just learned.

Rhythm Exercise 6

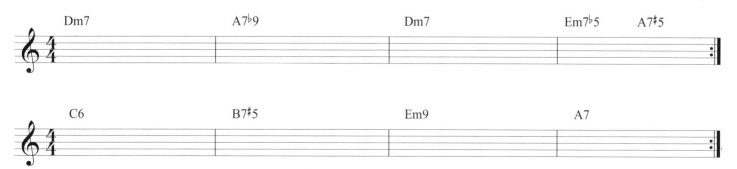

Progressions

Use this progression to learn the newer altered chords. It is also a review of the 9ths, 11ths, and 13ths presented. Also, consider style, rhtyhms and ensemble "kicks" that could be part of this chart. You can write rhythm ideas directly above or below the staff. Chord boxes are located below for your use if needed. Remember, voicings are used only when they *feel* familiar, when you have played them so many times that your fingers fall into them without thought.

It takes repetition and patience!

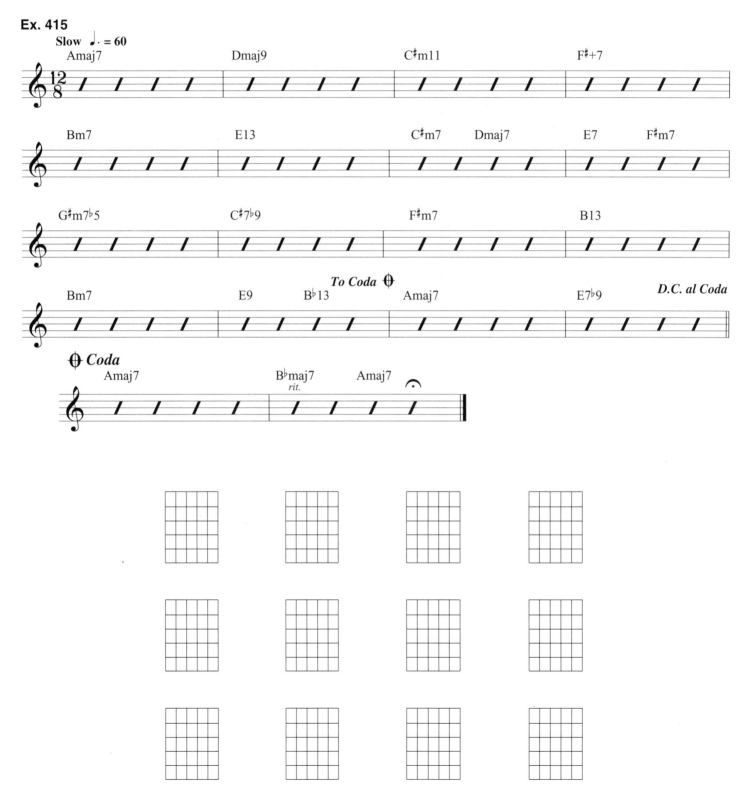

Ex. 415

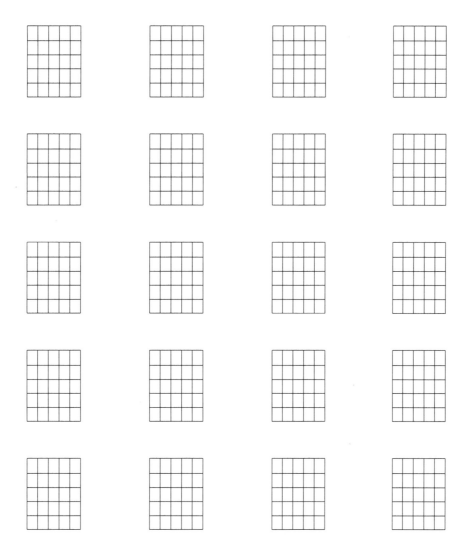

Notes:

Chapter Thirty-Two

Rhythm Control Exercises

Rhythm is ultimately the most important aspect of music. It is what reaches us first. When something is "correct" rhythmically, then we can easily relate to the melodic and harmonic aspects of the music. If it isn't correct then we have problems—as both a listener and player—relating to the music. We feel uncomfortable and don't hear as well. Having realized this, the non-drummer musician must set up things in his or her practice that will help cure any rhythmic "ills."

Here are some good exercises that should serve as daily practice to improve your feel for *time.* Expand upon these with your own ideas, and also observe what is going on in the music you listen to. Much practicing can be done simply by listening and imitating what you hear, then developing the ideas into some small practice routine. It goes without saying a metronome is necessary. However, to absorb a style and its way of emphasizing and working with rhythms, you must listen and imitate the masters in that style! Be consistent in your daily practice by always thinking *rhythm* in your playing and practicing. Use it when doing scales, arpeggios, and chord progressions, and also do pure rhythm studies to develop accuracy and relaxation.

To develop a strong sense of rhythm and confidence in your time, you must drill on figures that accent different parts (subdivisions) of the beat. A common technique of rhythmic syncopation is to place accents on the basic subdivision that changes from downbeat to up beat. Here it is at the eighth note level. Try to memorize each example and look away from the page, hearing and feeling the rhythm.

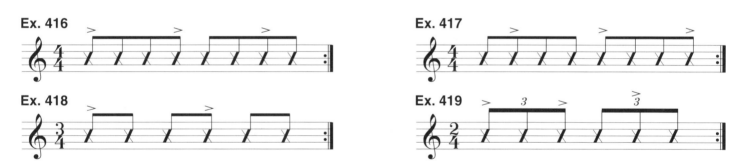

Here are the same accents at the sixteenth note level (twice as fast). Notice the relationship of sets of *threes* in the accents, to the sets of *fours* in the subdivision.

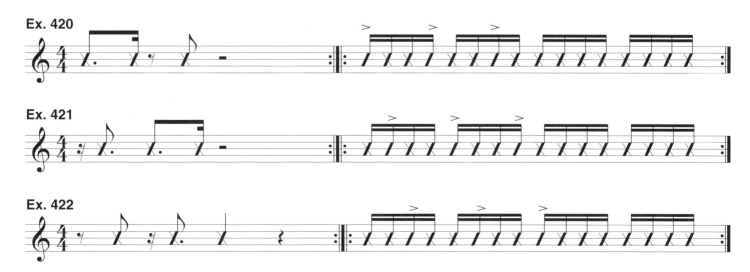

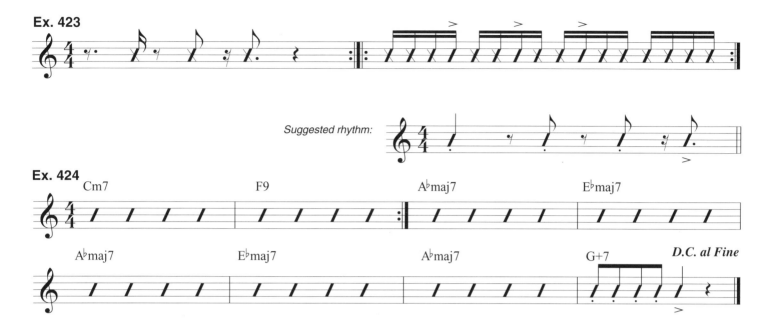

Ex. 423

Suggested rhythm:

Ex. 424

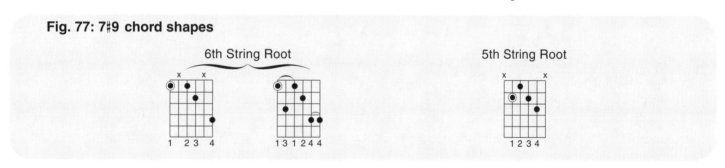

More Altered Dominant Chords

The 7♯9 is another common alteration. Learn it off of sixth and fifth string roots.

Fig. 77: 7♯9 chord shapes

6th String Root   5th String Root

Example 425 incorporates a syncopated sixteenth rhythm and a 7♯9 chord.

Suggested rhythm:

Ex. 425

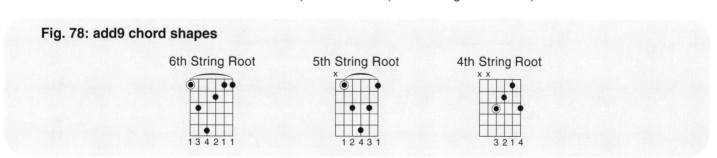

Add9 Chords

Add9 chords are contructed of a triad plus the ninth (second degree of scale).

Fig. 78: add9 chord shapes

6th String Root   5th String Root   4th String Root

Example 426 merges eighth note syncopations and add9 chords. Experiment with different voicings.

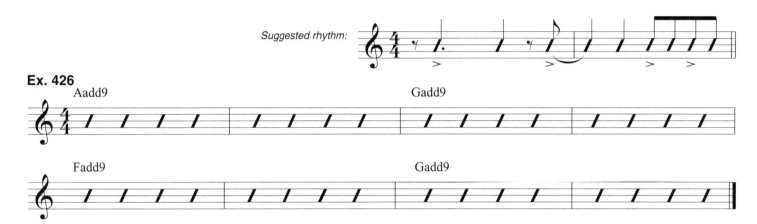

Ex. 426

Aadd9   Gadd9

Fadd9   Gadd9

Notes:

Chapter Thirty-Three

Objectives

- To learn ii-V-I progressions in major keys.
- To observe movement of individual voices and learn about basic voice leading principles.
- To play a tune based on ii-V-I progressions.

The ii-V-I Progression

After the I-IV-V progression (the most basic), the ii-V-I progression is the second most important and most common. The ii-V-I progression sounds so familiar because is uses the cycle of fifths (or fourths—moving down a fifth brings us to the same note as moving up a fourth). The cycle of fifths is the bass motion on which the entire diatonic system is based. The most basic movement of down a fifth (or up a fourth) is achieved by the movement of I to IV (C to F) and by the movement of V back to I (G7 to C). In the ii-V-I progression, this cycle movement happens twice in a row, from ii to V (Dm to G7) and from V to I (G7 to C).

Voice Leading

Voice leading implies we are looking at a note of a chord as being a seperate voice, which creates its own melody as we move from one chord to the next. The voice leading principles most common are:

- Common Tone and/or Closest Tone.
- Contrary Motion.
- Chromatic Movement.

The examples that follow will illustrate these principles, but you must observe the movement of the voices and try to create your own examples to truly understand and hear these principles.

Common Tone and Closest Tone

Here the idea is to not make a note (voice) move if it is common to both chords. If a note is not common to both chords, then it should move to the nearest or closest chord tone of the next chord. Observe where this occurs in each of the following examples.

Some of the examples may contain voicings not shown in the curriculum until now. Practice and memorize any that are new to you. Inversions, extensions, and alterations are also used. Below each example is a blank staff. Write the notes of each chord voicing on the staff and observe the voice-leading principles. Take your time in learning these examples in order to retain them. Practice them frequently and be sure to play in all the keys that seem practical on the instrument given each particular voicing.

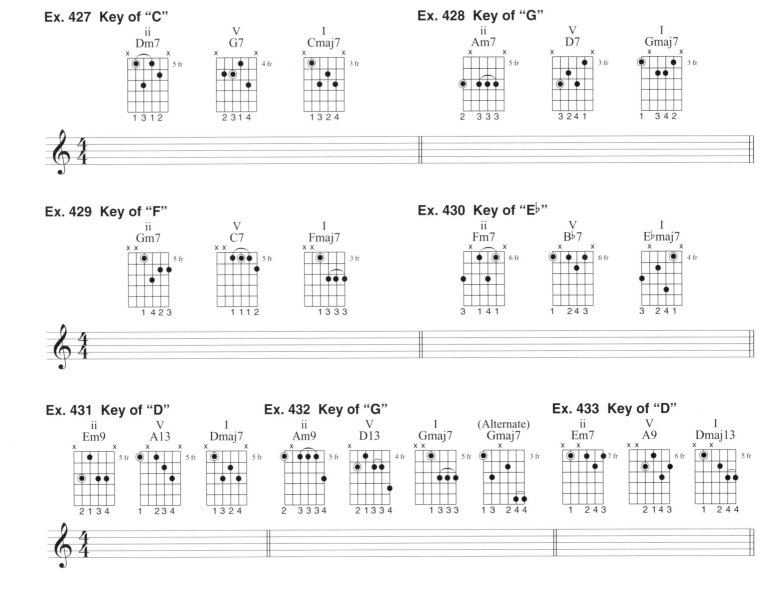

Ex. 427 Key of "C"

ii
Dm7

V
G7

I
Cmaj7

Ex. 428 Key of "G"

ii
Am7

V
D7

I
Gmaj7

Ex. 429 Key of "F"

ii
Gm7

V
C7

I
Fmaj7

Ex. 430 Key of "E♭"

ii
Fm7

V
B♭7

I
E♭maj7

Ex. 431 Key of "D"

ii
Em9

V
A13

I
Dmaj7

Ex. 432 Key of "G"

ii
Am9

V
D13

I
Gmaj7

(Alternate)
Gmaj7

Ex. 433 Key of "D"

ii
Em7

V
A9

I
Dmaj13

Contrary Motion

Contrary motion happens when the direction of the lowest and highest notes of the chord are moving in opposite directions. This effect is always a good one. It gives the sense of expanding and contracting in the melody and bass line which gives the listener something interesting to track with the ear. Observe the examples, noting the use of extensions and alterations.

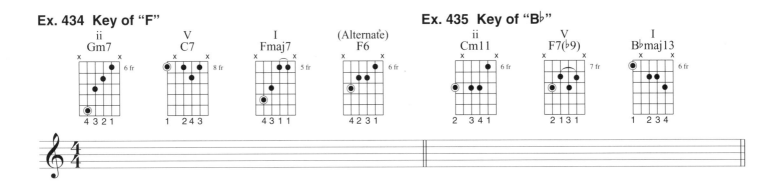

Ex. 434 Key of "F"

ii
Gm7

V
C7

I
Fmaj7

(Alternate)
F6

Ex. 435 Key of "B♭"

ii
Cm11

V
F7(♭9)

I
B♭maj13

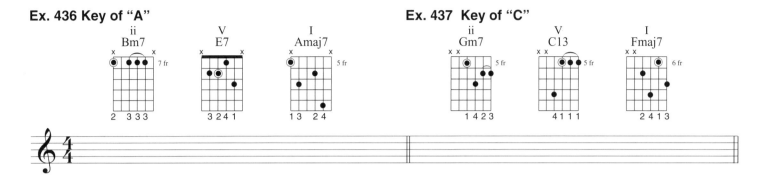

Ex. 436 Key of "A"

ii	V	I
Bm7	E7	Amaj7

Ex. 437 Key of "C"

ii	V	I
Gm7	C13	Fmaj7

Chormatic Movement

Chromatic movement involves the use of alterations in the dominant V chord. The tension created by alteration is resolved when the chromatic tone moves by a half step to the I chord. This usually involves extensions and their alterations, such as 9–11–13 as well as ♭9, ♯9, ♯11♭5, and ♭13♯5.

NOTE: This priniciple will be explored further in the next chapter.

Chart

The following song is an example of the use of ii-V-I. The progression is made up almost entirely of this harmonic movement, but it modulates keys to keep things fresh. Try to use the above examples and/or make up some moves of your own. Look for more tunes that employ the ii-V-I and use these same moves. Use extensions and alterations at your discretion. If the chart says a 7th chord, try a 9th or 13th chord or alteration to hear if it works. There is no melody, so experiment!

Laura's Sister

Ex. 438

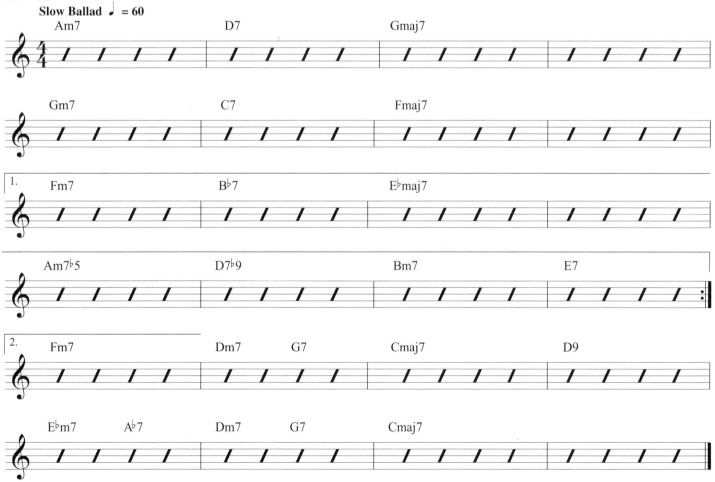

Chapter Thirty-Four

34

Triplet Strumming

In previous chapters we worked on sixteenth note rhythms, the objective being to achieve a relaxed, even stroke, and steady time. In this chapter we will continue to work on strumming, using triplet patterns. Remember to practice with a metronome or drum machine but don't rely on them. You must develop your own sense of time and groove.

- Play these exercises while muting with the fretting hand (no sounding chord).
- Focus on being relaxed and even as you feel and hear these triplet patterns.
- Notice the picking directions and optional picking patterns.

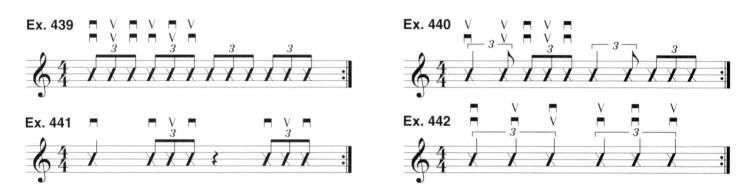

One and Two Bar Patterns

Play these one- and two-bar figures on any one chord (i.e., E9, Dm7, or A13, etc.), and be able to play them from memory. Note: X on the slash indicates muted attack. Slash indicates sounding chord.

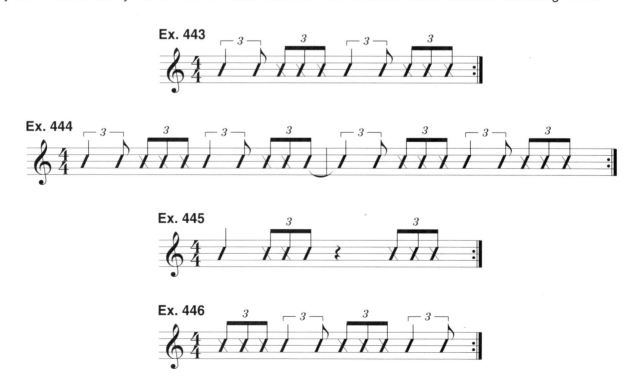

130

Chart

In the following chart, there are some new voicings introduced. The C/D, E♭/F, and D/E chords are all the same chord type, voiced exactly the same way. Another name for these slash chords is dominant 9sus4. Play the chart with a couple different triplet grooves. Work on a relaxed triplet feel and observe and learn any new voicings.

Laura's Other Sister

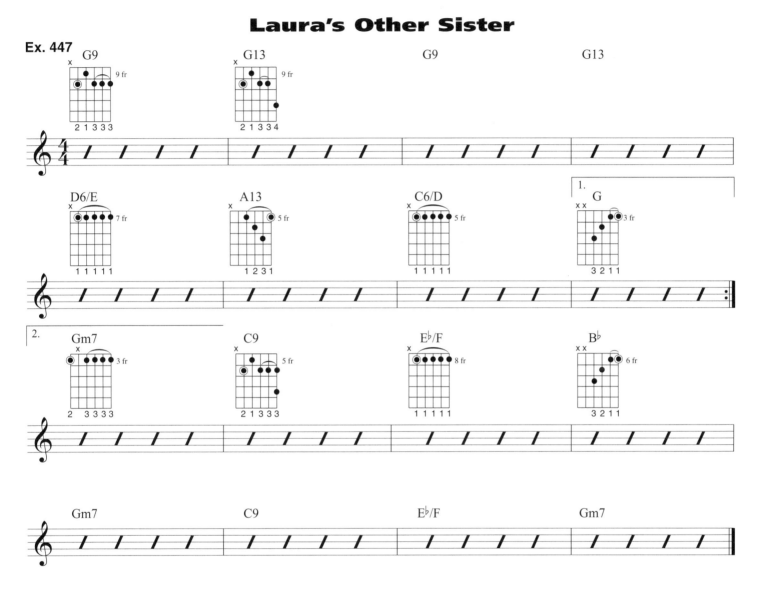

Practice Tips:

- Learn all ii-V-I shapes. (Some may seem difficult at first).

- Practice daily to maintain your flexibility. The more shapes your fingers must change to, the more independent your fingers become.

- New chords need individual attention as well as part of the ii-V-I move.

- Pay attention to the melody line that is the top note of each chord. Sing it!

- Put these moves directly into songs and common progressions.

- Eventually play all these moves in all keys!

More ii-V-Is

Again, play each ii-V-I progression and write out the voicings on the staff, noting the voice leading.

Ex. 448 Key of "G"

ii	V	I
Am7	D7#9	Gmaj7

Ex. 449 Key of "D"

ii	V	I
Em9	A7#5	Dmaj9

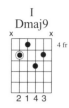

Ex. 450 Key of "D"

ii	V	I
Em7	A7#5#9	Dmaj7

Ex. 451 Key of "F"

ii	V	I
Gm7	C7b5	F6

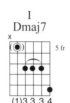

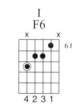

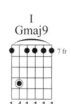
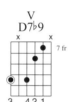
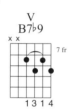

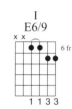

Ex. 452 Key of "G"

ii	V	I
Am7	D7b9	Gmaj9

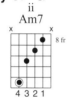

Ex. 453 Key of "E"

ii	V	I
F#m7	B7b9	E6/9

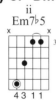

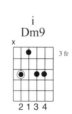

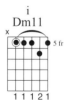

Minor ii-V-is

Minor ii-V-is have a m7b5 for the ii, dominant 7th for the V, and of course a minor chord for the i.

Ex. 454 Key of "Dm"

ii	V	i
Em7b5	A7#5	Dm9

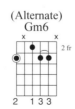

Ex. 455 Key of "Dm"

ii	V	i
Em7b5	A7#9(#5)	Dm11

Ex. 456 Key of "Gm"

ii	V	i	(Alternate)
Am7b5	D7b9	Gm7	Gm6

Chapter Thirty-Five

Creating Parts

In the next few chapters we will look at different ways the rhythm guitarist can create his/her own "part" and interpret a given harmony. This is done primarily through the use of triads and 7th chords along with double-stops (two notes at once) and single-note melodies. When you combine rhythm patterns with ideas based on any of these concepts, you can help define certain styles and grooves with your rhythm playing.

Double Stops in Thirds

First let's look at double stops: specifically thirds. (Any interval can be a double stop: thirds, sixths, and fourths are the most common). Any combination of double stops is legitimate if it:

- Interprets the chord change (conveying the appropriate major or minor sound, etc.).
- Has a solid rhythmic foundation.
- Sounds good! (subjective, stylistic musical reasons).

Double stops create small harmonic textures that compliment the overall sound and are used in a supportive role. You should practice with a live rhythm section and/or tapes (bass lines, drum patterns, etc.) to explore this type of chordal texturing.

Play diatonic thirds as double stops on the top two strings in the harmonized C major scale below.

Ex. 316

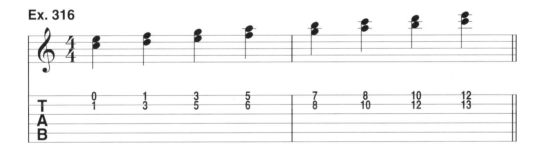

Play diatonic thirds on the second and third strings.

Ex. 317

Note: Eventually, you want to know these shapes (3rds) all over the neck, including the other string sets (3 and 4, 4 and 5, 5 and 6).

"Basic Moves"

In the following exercises, thirds are used with rhythms to outline the sound of each chord. Think about different bass lines that might go with these parts. What about drums? Alternate chords?

Ex. 457 *Rock*

Amaj7 (or F#m7)

Ex. 458 *Funky*

Dmaj9

Ex. 459 *Funk/Ballad*

Cmaj9   Fm9   G7sus4   G+7

Ex. 460 *Pop*

Emaj7   A9sus4   B9sus4

Emaj7   A9sus4   B9sus4

Ex. 461 *Latin/Jazz*

Bm7   B♭maj7

Ex. 462 *Blues*

G   Gm or C9

*Key signature denotes G Mixolydian.

Ex. 463 *Funk*

Dmaj9   Bm7   Em9   A7

Ex. 464 *Jazz ending on ballad*

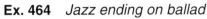

Create a rhythm part using *thirds* for the following progression. Think of style.

Ex. 465

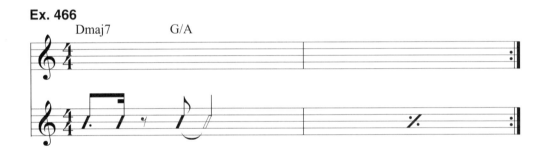

Ex. 466

Ex. 467

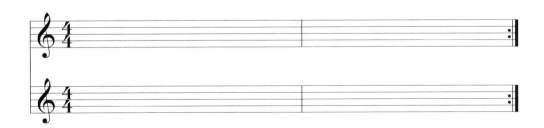

Now write your own chords and rhythms.

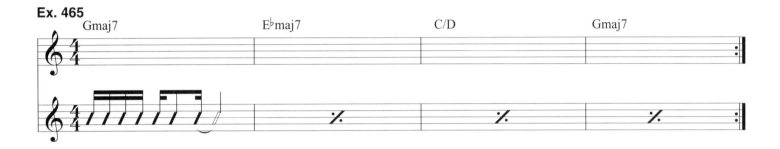

Chapter Thirty-Six

36

More Double Stops

In this chapter, we will look at double stops built on the intervals of fourths and sixths. Also we'll observe the relationship between relative major and minor. These examples are meant to show a typical use of these intervals but again the student should strive to adapt them to his or her style and also write your own, based on some of these concepts. The first exercises are based on the pure interval shapes that occur on the top two sets of strings. Repeated practice in different keys is mandatory if you want to be able to use these and create your own ideas for different progressions and songs. Examples are shown in the key of "C" but make sure you transpose them. Fingerings for the sixths may change for different examples so be sure you experiment with the fingering. Also work on muting the unwanted (dead) strings.

Double Stops in Fourths

Fourth intervals are also common double stops. The shape is easily played with one finger. All of the shapes that go through the harmonized scale are perfect fourths, except one, which is an augmented fourth. Which two notes of the scale makeup the augmented fourth?

Ex. 316

Ex. 317

In the example below, first observe how many different fourths are needed, then put them into the rhythm indicated.

Ex. 470

In example 471, first the melody "lick" is in D major, then D minor (the parallel minor). In order to retain the perfect fourth interval sound, we didn't just change the third (F♯) to a minor third (F natural), but rather, moved the "lick" up a minor third (one and one-half steps) to what would appear to be an F major lick. But it now works as a D minor idea. This uses the relative minor concept. *Note: Ideas are based in major usually work also on their relative minor and vice versa.)*

In the next example, the same lick is being used over the relative minor. First we have basically fourths, in a pentatonic sound, played over the major I–V–IV. Then the same idea is used over the relative minor key, I–V–IV. Hear how it sounds good over both!

Write some of your own ideas using fourths!

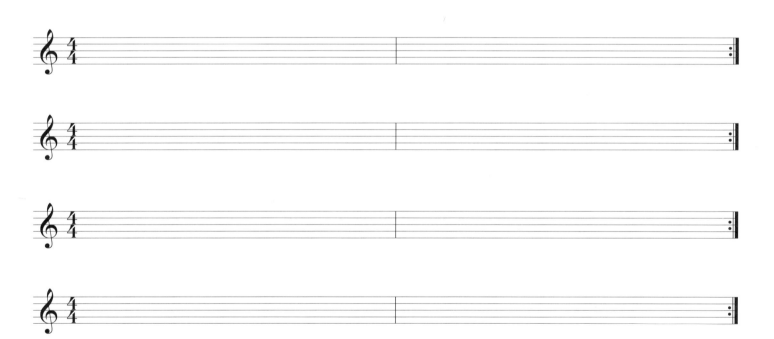

Double Stops in Sixths

Sixth intervals can be played on adjacent strings or by skipping a string, which requires you mute the string in between. Experiment with both ways. However, these exercises are all written with the string skip shape in mind. Observe the pattern of major and minor sixths that is created. The following examples can be used in C major (and the common modes: A Aeolian, D Dorian, and G Mixolydian).

Ex. 473

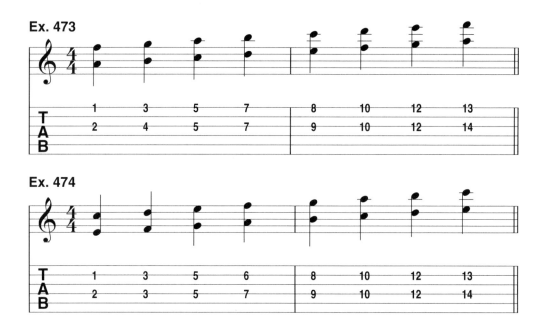

Ex. 474

Here's a simple idea that works well on the chords indicated. What chord tones are involved with each sixth interval, and how do they relate to the chord?

Ex. 475

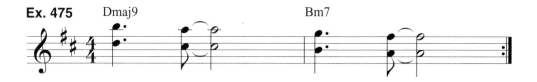

In the next example, the same lick is starting from a different place each time. All are on a G7 chord, and the harmonization is Mixolydian. They could be used together (different guitars) or played one after another.

Ex. 476

3rd on top

*Key signature reflects G Mixolydian

5th on top

♭*7th on top*

Play this one with straight eighth note power chords. Notice the changed note (F) to adapt to the next chord.

Exercises

Here are some simple harmonic movements (progressions) you can experiment with using fourths and sixths. These are typical I–IV or I–V moves. Don't forget to make up your own chords as well. Also change the time signature if you want.

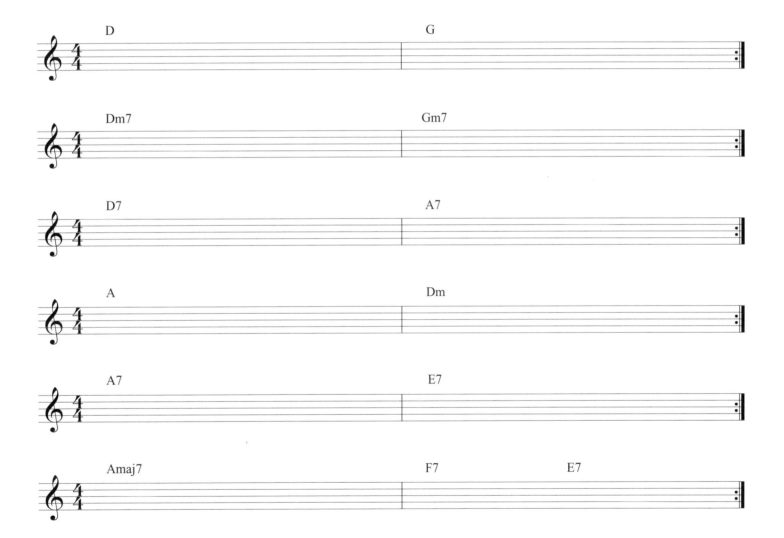

Notes:

Chapter Thirty-Seven

37

Single-Note Rhythm Parts

Oftentimes, if a second guitar part is needed in the rhythm section, the guitarist is called on to play some single-notes that serve a percusive function. Single-note rhythm parts are generally improvised. They are a little touch added to the overall sound and should be played with strong time and short, catchy phrases! These single notes are being used in a rhythmic way, so few notes are needed—two, three, or four notes are plenty. The trick is to set up a motif, or repetitive type of idea.

The first step would be to start with only one note and improvise rhythmically. Then try just two notes, then three notes, etc. The key is playing with short, stabbing notes that will pop out in a mix. The strumming hand should be relaxed and percussive in its attack! Muting unwanted strings with the fretboard hand (left for most of us) also requires repetition and practice as you experiment with different melodies.

The most common two note group in pop styles is the *root* to the ♭*7*. Work with it in a variety of rhythms and get used to muting with the left hand and scratching with the right hand.

Try these phrases on Am or A7.

Applications

The next few examples show a melody line over specific chords. Notice the relationship between the single-note lines and the chords they are played over.

Here the chords go down a major third but the line goes up a fourth.

Ex. 484

A "question/answer? type of phrase appears in exercise 485.

Ex. 485

Here is a simple pentatonic melody over chords that change keys!

Ex. 486

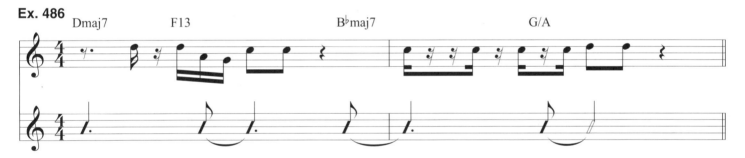

In the chart below, figure out four one-measure phrases to fit each chord type and string them together in this modal progression.

Ex. 487

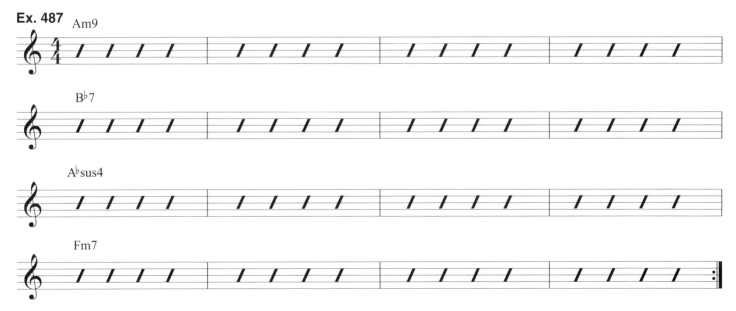

Press

Musicians Institute Press

is the official series of Southern California's renowned music school, Musicians Institute.

MI instructors, some of the finest musicians in the world, share their vast knowledge and experience with you – no matter what your current level.

For guitar, bass, drums, vocals, and keyboards, **MI Press** offers the finest music curriculum for higher learning through a variety of series:

FOR MORE INFORMATION, SEE YOUR LOCAL MUSIC DEALER,
OR WRITE TO:

HAL•LEONARD®
CORPORATION

7777 W. BLUEMOUND RD. P.O. BOX 13819 MILWAUKEE, WI 53213

ESSENTIAL CONCEPTS
Designed from MI core curriculum programs.

Bass Playing Techniques
by Alexis Sklarevski
00695207 . . . .$14.95

Guitar Improvisation
by Dan Gilbert & Beth Marlis
00695190 . . . .$17.95

Harmony & Theory
by Keith Wyatt & Carl Schroeder
00695161 . . . .$14.95

Music Reading for Guitar
by David Oakes
00695192 . . . .$14.95

Sight Singing
by Mike Campbell
00695195 . . . .$14.95

Music Reading for Bass
by Wendy Wrehovcsik
00695203 . . . .$14.95

Music Reading for Keyboard
by Larry Steelman
00695205 . . . .$14.95

Ear Training
by Keith Wyatt, Carl Schroeder, & Joe Elliot
00695198 . . . .$17.95

Keyboard Voicings
by Kevin King
00695209 . . . .$14.95

Bass Fretboard Basics
by Paul Farnen
00695201 . . . .$14.95

Rhythm Guitar
by Bruce Buckingham & Eric Paschal
00695188 Book/CD $17.95

MASTER CLASS
Designed from MI elective courses.

Rock Lead Basics
by Danny Gill & Nick Nolan
00695144 Book/CD $14.95

Jazz Guitar Improvisation
by Sid Jacobs
00695128 Book/CD $17.95

Jazz Improvisation
by Dave Pozzi
00695135 Book/CD $17.95

Walking Bass
by Bob Magnusson
00695168 Book/CD $17.95

Blues Bass
by Alexis Sklarevski
00695150 Book/CD $17.95

Guitar Playing Techniques
by David Oakes
00695171 . . . .$12.95

Rock Lead Guitar Techniques
by Nick Nolan & Danny Gill
00695146 Book/CD $16.95

PRIVATE LESSONS
Tackle a variety of topics "one-on-one" with MI faculty instructors.

Arpeggios for Bass
by Dave Keif
00695133 . . . .$12.95

Chart Reading for Drummers
00695129 . . . .$19.95

The Diminished Scale for Guitar
by Jean Marc Belkad
00695227 . . . .$7.95

Encyclopedia of Reading Rhythms
by Gary Hess
00695145 Book/CD $19.95

Guitar Basics
by Bruce Buckingham
00695134 Book/CD $14.95

Harmonics for Guitar
by Jamie Findlay
00695169 . . . .$7.95

Lead Sheet Bible
by Robin Randall
00695130 Book/CD $17.95

Modern Approach to Jazz, Rock & Fusion Guitar
by Jean March-Belkadi
00695143 Book/CD $14.95

Odd Meter Bassics
by Dino Monoxelos
00695170 Book/CD $14.95

Open String Chords for Guitar
by Jamie Findlay
00695172 . . . .$7.95

Salsa Hanon
by Peter Deneff
00695226 . . . .$9.95

Working the Inner Clock for Drumset
by Phil Maturano
00695127 . . . .$16.95

Prices, contents, and availability subject to change without notice. Some products may not be available outside of the U.S.A.

0997